The Education Center®

The IDEA MAGAZINE FOR TEACHERS®

MAILBOX®

2007–2008 YEARBOOK

The Education Center, Inc.
Greensboro, North Carolina

The Mailbox® 2007–2008 Preschool Yearbook

Managing Editor, *The Mailbox* Magazine: Kimberly Brugger-Murphy

Editorial Team: Becky S. Andrews, Diane Badden, Kimberley Bruck, Karen A. Brudnak, Kitty Campbell, Pam Crane, Lynette Dickerson, Lynn Drolet, Sarah Foreman, Margaret Freed (COVER ARTIST), Karen Brewer Grossman, Tazmen Hansen, Marsha Heim, Lori Z. Henry, Amy Kirtley-Hill, Dorothy C. McKinney, Brenda Miner, Sharon Murphy, Jennifer Nunn, Tina Petersen, Mark Rainey, Greg D. Rieves, Kelly Robertson, Hope Rodgers, Eliseo De Jesus Santos II, Rebecca Saunders, Donna K. Teal, Joshua Thomas, Zane Williard

ISBN10 1-56234-857-4
ISBN13 978-156234-857-1
ISSN 1088-5536

Printed in the United States of America.

The Education Center, Inc.
P.O. Box 9753
Greensboro, NC 27429-0753

Look for *The Mailbox® 2008–2009 Preschool Yearbook* in the summer of 2009. The Education Center, Inc., is the publisher of *The Mailbox*®, *Teacher's Helper*®, *The Mailbox*® BOOKBAG®, and *Learning*® magazines, as well as other fine products. Look for these wherever quality teacher materials are sold, call 1-800-714-7991, or visit www.themailbox.com.

Contents

Departments

Features

Book Units

Center Units

Literacy Units

Math Units

Thematic Units

Arts & Crafts for Little Hands

Arts & Crafts for Little Hands

Puffy Apples

This three-dimensional fruit project is perfect for back-to-school! Cut out a construction paper leaf, stem, and worm and set them aside. Gently stir red, yellow, or green paint into a mixture of glue and nonmentholated shaving cream. Place spoonfuls of the mixture on a brightly colored sheet of construction paper. Then use the spoon to spread the mixture so that it resembles an apple. Slide the leaf, stem, and worm into the mixture. Allow a few days for drying time. This awesome apple looks terrific displayed on a bulletin board.

Color Rolling

This simple process-oriented art results in a colorful masterpiece! Wrap a rolling pin in aluminum foil and roll it through a cookie sheet of paint. Then roll it over a 12" x 18" sheet of construction paper. Repeat the process with other colors of paint until a desired effect is achieved. Throughout the year, repeat this activity with colors related to the seasons.

Janet Boyce
Cokato, MN

Foil Prints

In advance, mold pieces of aluminum foil to make simple stampers. Choose a stamper and gently press an end into a shallow pan of paint. Then make a print on a sheet of construction paper. Continue in the same way with other stampers and colors of paint. If desired, mount the project on a larger piece of paper and add foil embellishments.

Janet Boyce
Cokato, MN

Splendid Shoelaces

Cut various shoelaces into six-inch lengths. Clip a clothespin to the end of each prepared shoelace. Then wrap tape around the clothespin to keep it closed. Grip a clothespin and drag the accompanying shoelace through a shallow container of paint. Then drag the paint-covered lace over a piece of paper. Continue with other shoelaces and different colors of paint to make a delightful design. If desired, trim the finished paper into the shape of a shoe and embellish it as desired.

Janet Boyce

Arts & Crafts for Little Hands

Lovely Lights

These brilliant lights will brighten up everyone's holiday! Tint white corn syrup with neon or regular food coloring. Then dip the back of a spoon into the corn syrup and press the spoon onto a blank sentence strip, rolling it slightly to create the shape shown. Repeat the process with other colors of tinted syrup. Allow the project to dry for 48 hours. Then use a green marker to draw a cord to connect the lights. These lovely lights make a terrific bulletin board border!

Janet Boyce
Cokato, MN

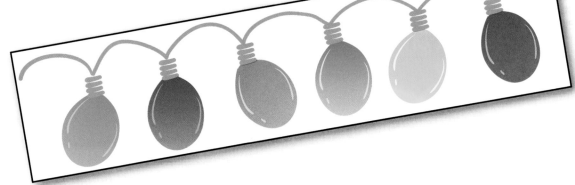

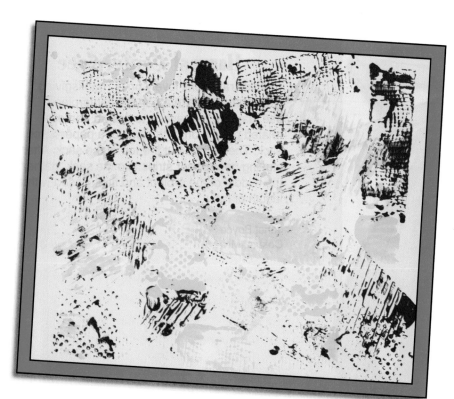

Candle Prints

Here's a fun printmaking activity that's just perfect for a Hanukkah or Kwanzaa celebration! Gather a supply of candles that are ribbed or textured. Then place each candle next to a shallow container of tempera paint. Roll a candle in the corresponding paint and then roll it on a sheet of construction paper or newsprint. Continue in the same way with the remaining candles and containers of paint until a desired effect is achieved.

Janet Boyce

A Tasty Home

These cute holiday centerpieces look good enough to eat! Decorate a lunch bag so it resembles a house. Then stuff the bag with newspaper strips and staple it closed. Attach a roof cutout to the bag. Then decorate the bag with cotton batting frosting and cutouts that resemble candy. When a desired effect is achieved, glue the bag to a paper plate and then attach gingerbread-man cutouts to the finished house.

Jodi and Linda Remington
Busy Day Child Care
Okemos, MI

Candy Cane Cradle

Here's an adorable Christmas craft! Color or paint a white candy cane cutout with red stripes. With the candy cane upside down, attach a star cutout and curling ribbon to the top of the project. Glue Spanish moss to the bottom of the project to create a manger. Then draw a picture of a baby, cut it out, and attach it to the moss.

Phyllis Prestridge
First United Methodist Church Early Learning Center
Amory, MS

Statue of Liberty Pattern
Use with "Star-Studded Statue" on page 17.

TEC41037

BULLETIN BOARDS AND DISPLAYS

The Preschool Class, Starring...

This stellar display is simple to make! Attach two lengths of fabric to opposite ends of your bulletin board and then gather each length with ribbon so that the fabric resembles theater curtains. Attach a photo of each child to a different star cutout and personalize the cutouts. Then mount the stars and title shown on the bulletin board.

Victoria Aguilar, Westminster Presbyterian Preschool, Westlake Village, CA

Can You Spot Your Name?

This door display is "paws-itively" adorable! Use a white gel pen or correction pen to write each child's name on a different black spot cutout. Then attach the spots to a large white dog cutout. After laminating the dog for durability, attach the dog to the inside of your classroom door. Finally, mount the title shown above the dog. When youngsters are waiting at the door, encourage them to spot their names!

Heather Campbell
Hopewell Country Day School
Pennington, NJ

Use bulletin board paper to make a large tree cutout, or obtain a premade tree cutout. Attach the tree to a wall along with the title shown. Each month throughout the school year, have youngsters add to the tree seasonal shapes labeled with numbers, letters, shapes, and concepts they've learned. By the end of the year, you'll have a terrific visual that shows the many things students have learned in the classroom.

Sarah Booth
Messiah Nursery School
South Williamsport, PA

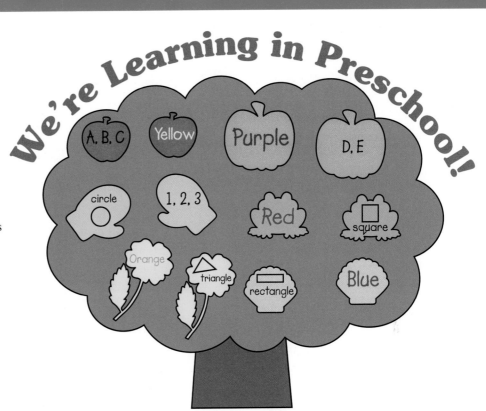

To make this birthday board, make two beehive cutouts for each month in the year. Staple each pair of cutouts together, leaving an opening. Write a different month on each hive and then stuff the hives with crumpled newspaper strips. Display the hives in order. Then have each child color a bee cutout personalized with his name and birthday. (See page 255 for a bee pattern.) Attach each bee to the appropriate hive. Then add the title shown to the display.

Bonnie Martin, Hopewell Country Day School, Pennington, NJ

You'll see oodles of grins when youngsters and classroom visitors view this cute display! Have each child paint two or three cardboard tubes brown. When the paint is dry, attach the tubes to a bulletin board to resemble a fence. Next, have each child stuff a paper lunch sack with newspaper strips. Twist the top of the bag and tape it in place; then have students paint and decorate their bags as shown. Add a pipe cleaner vine to each jack-o'-lantern. Then attach the jack-o'-lanterns to the board and add the title shown.

Melissa A. Humphries and Tammie Looney, Covington, VA

This fun display is a hoot! Cut out a brown construction paper copy of the owl mask on page 272 for each youngster; then cut out the eyeholes. If desired, have each child glue craft feathers to her mask. Then instruct her to tape a jumbo craft stick to the mask to make a handle. Have each student hold her mask to her face while you take her photograph. Display the photos along with night sky decorations and the title shown.

adapted from an idea by Shelley Barney and
  Cary Howes
New Athens Elementary
New Athens, IL

To make this sweet display, have youngsters make a variety of candy-related crafts. To make a lollipop, have each student squeeze white glue on a construction paper circle in a swirling pattern. Then invite him to shake glitter over the glue. When the glue is dry, instruct him to tape a jumbo craft stick to the project. To make a chocolate kiss, have each child glue squares of aluminum foil to a kiss-shaped cutout. Then invite her to glue a paper tag to the craft. Mount the crafts on a display decorated and titled as shown.

Noelle Lawrence
Pixie Preschool and Kindergarten
Spotswood, NJ

Color and cut out an enlarged copy of the turkey pattern on page 31. Have each child attach an orange triangle cutout to a slightly larger brown triangle cutout to make a slice of pumpkin pie. Encourage her to glue a cotton ball (whipped cream) to the top of the pie. Then have her glue the pie slice and a plastic fork to a colorful disposable plate. Mount the plates around the turkey. Then add the title shown to this nifty display.

Sarah Booth, Messiah Nursery School, South Williamsport, PA
Freida Fields, First United Methodist Church Weekday School, Hendersonville, NC

Preschool Postage Is First-Class!

Pam Adam Kiesha Mitch Tim

Tony Dawn Susie Don Kim

Try this cute idea for a first-class display! Have each child draw a self-portrait on a supersize stamp cutout. Mount each stamp on a sheet of paper in a contrasting color. Then display the projects on a board titled as shown.

Kelly Hoffman, C. M. Bradley, Warrenton, VA

Time for Spring!

Chase Lacy Davis Colby Abby Maddie

Bring a touch of springtime into your classroom with this display! Make a construction paper clockface for each child. Have him glue crumpled tissue paper squares around the edge of the clock. Then encourage him to color and cut out a copy of a bird pattern from page 196. Display the clocks and birds on a wall with the title "Time for Spring!"

Erin McGinness
Great New Beginnings Early Learning Center
Newark, DE

Celebrate Dr. Seuss's birthday with this unique display honoring the Cat in the Hat! Paint the ball and toes of each child's foot black; then paint the remaining portion of her foot with red and white stripes. Press her foot onto a sheet of white construction paper. After the paint dries, help her cut out her footprint. Then have her cut eyes and a nose from paper scraps and glue them in place. Have her glue crinkle strips to the project to make whiskers and draw a mouth with a black marker. Display the resulting cats with the title shown.

Frankie McNair
Westwood Elementary School
Abbeville, SC

Give each child three construction paper copies of the card patterns on page 32. Have her color the hearts on each card. Then encourage her to brush glue over the hearts and sprinkle red glitter over the glue. Help her write her name on a hand cutout. Then mount each set of three cards to a board above the corresponding hand. Add the title shown to finish this nifty display.

Sarah Booth, Messiah Nursery School, South Williamsport, PA

Many Green and Speckled Frogs Sat on a Speckled Log Reading Some Most Terrific Books!

To make this adorable display, have a child use a toothbrush to spatter paint on a frog cutout (pattern on page 33). Help her fold a rectangular piece of construction paper so it resembles a book and then attach it to the front of the frog so it looks as if it's reading. Mount the finished projects on a bulletin board decorated and titled as shown.

Karen Rumolo, Pixie Preschool and Kindergarten, Spotswood, NJ

Celebrate Cinco de Mayo!

Celebrate Cinco de Mayo with a unique display of sombreros! For each child, hot-glue a paper cup to a paper plate. Provide several containers of colorful paint, along with sequins, pom-poms, and glitter. Invite each child to paint her sombrero and then decorate it as desired. Attach a length of colorful ribbon to the back of each plate. Then display the projects with the title shown.

Viviana Rada
A Touch of the Future Bilingual Preschool
Lutz, FL

Have each child make green fingerprints on a leaf cutout so they resemble a caterpillar. Encourage him to draw antennae and facial details on his caterpillar. Then have him punch holes in the leaf. Mount a paper tree to a wall; then attach the leaves to the tree and title the display "Crunch, Munch! Leaves for Lunch!"

Amy Aloi, Bollman Bridge RECC, Jessup, MD

Crunch, Munch! Leaves for Lunch!

To make these personalized seed packets, have each child attach flower stickers to a construction paper frame labeled as shown. Encourage her to tape a photo of herself and a craft stick to the frame. Mount the seed packets to a board decorated with yarn earthworms and bunny cutouts. Add the title "Watch Us Grow!"

Barbara Carothers Ulmer
Allisonville Christian Church Preschool, Indianapolis, IN

Share healthy snack recipes with parents using this adorable display! Mount a plastic tablecloth on a bulletin board and title the board as shown. Attach a basket cutout to the board, leaving the top of the basket open, and stock it with healthy recipes for parents to take home. Then have each child color a bear cutout and attach to one of its paws a cutout depicting a healthy food item. Mount the bears around the basket.

Cindy Lawson, Family Daycare, Amboy, IL

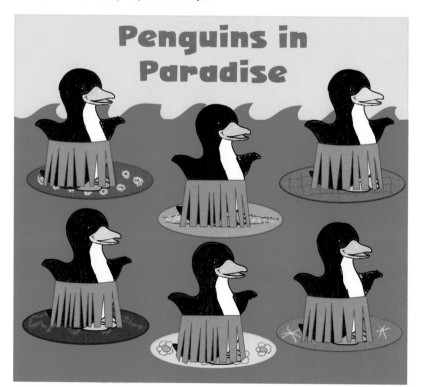

To make this adorable display, have each child color a tagboard penguin cutout. (See page 34 for a pattern.) Then have him fringe-cut a piece of green construction paper (grass skirt) and attach it to his penguin. Have him glue his penguin to a surfboard cutout. Mount the finished projects to a piece of blue bulletin board paper. Attach the paper to a wall and add the title shown.

Kim Dessel, Pixie Preschool and Kindergarten
Spotswood, NJ

TEC41033

Card Patterns

Use with "Hands Down, You've Won Our Hearts!" on page 27.

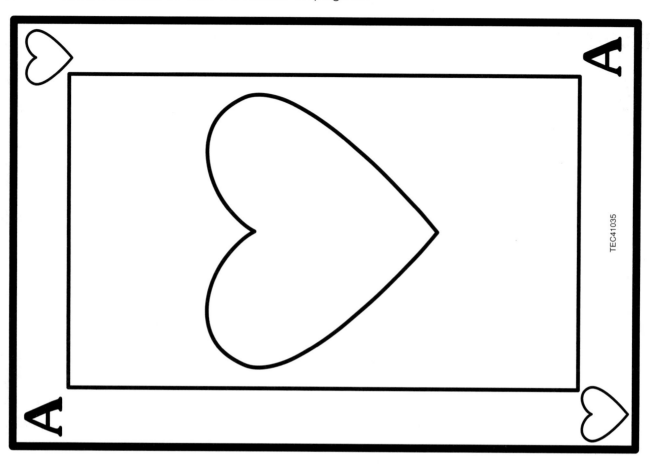

TEC41035

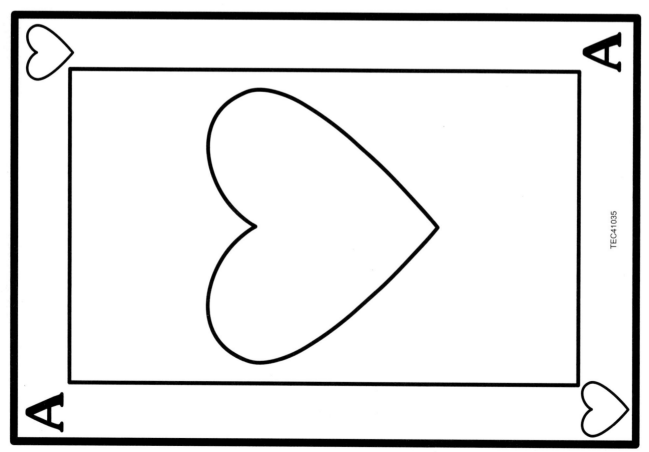

TEC41035

TEC41036

Penguin Pattern
Use with "Penguins in Paradise" on page 30.

TEC41037

BUSY HANDS

Busy Hands

Seasonal Explorations for Little Hands

Begin the school year with this fun collection of fine-motor activities!

ideas contributed by Colleen Jones, Hirsch Elementary, Spring, TX

SCHOOL BUS TRACKS

Place a supply of play dough at a table along with a toy school bus. A youngster flattens a large piece of dough. Then she "drives" the bus through the play dough and observes the fascinating tire tracks left behind.

CRAYON HUNT

Fill a container with rice that's been dyed a variety of colors. Hide crayons in the rice. Then provide access to a container and a strainer with holes that are large enough for the rice to pass through. A youngster uses the strainer to remove the crayons from the rice; then he places the crayons in the container.

HUNGRY ANTS

Attach a supersize picnic basket cutout to a tabletop. Provide glue and black mini pom-poms. A youngster visits the table and glues three pom-poms on the basket so the pom-poms resemble an ant. He continues adding ants to the basket. When each child has had a chance to add to the project, draw legs on each ant and attach the basket to a wall in your classroom.

CLEAN-SHAVEN DAD

Laminate a simple drawing of a face. Place the drawing at a table along with large craft sticks, baby wipes, and a bowl of nonmentholated shaving cream. A child visits the center, uses her fingers to smooth shaving cream onto the face, and then "shaves" it off with a craft stick. She uses a baby wipe to clean any remaining shaving cream from the face. Now that's a smooth shave!

TWIG DESIGNS

Program several large sheets of paper with letters, numbers, shapes, or outlines of objects such as a house or a boat. Then provide access to a supply of small twigs. A child places twigs along a desired outline or uses the twigs to create designs of his own.

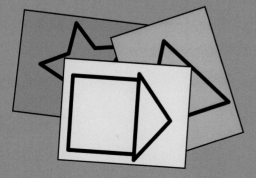

Busy Hands

Seasonal Explorations for Little Hands

Autumn leaves, harvest veggies, and turkey tracks! Your little ones are sure to be batty for these fall-themed explorations!

ideas contributed by Janet Boyce, Cokato, MN

TURKEY TRACKS

When youngsters make prints with a slightly altered drinking straw, the results are these fantastic turkey tracks! Cut a sturdy drinking straw in half; then make four lengthwise snips in the end of each straw half and remove one of the resulting flaps. Bend the remaining flaps back, and the result resembles a turkey leg and foot. Attach a length of paper to a table. Then place the straw halves at the table along with a shallow pan of paint. A youngster presses a straw into the paint and then makes prints on the paper. Look at all the turkey tracks!

JUST HANGING AROUND

Make several bat cutouts and place them in a basket along with a supply of spring-style clothespins. Secure a length of clothesline in your classroom. Then place the basket nearby. A child clips the bats to the clothesline so they are hanging upside down.

Ada Goren
Winston-Salem, NC

38

COOPERATIVE CORNUCOPIA

Draw and cut out a simple cornucopia from brown bulletin board paper. Attach the cornucopia to a tabletop. Place gardening catalogs and grocery store circulars at the table and provide access to glue sticks. Students cut out pictures of vegetables, fruits, nuts, and berries. Then they glue the pictures to the cornucopia. When each student has had several opportunities to contribute to the project, display it in your classroom.

LENGTHS OF LEAVES

Take youngsters outside to collect a variety of leaves. Place youngsters' leaves in a container. Then attach a length of packing tape to a tabletop with the sticky side facing up. Put the container of leaves nearby. Little ones visit the center and press leaves against the tape. Replace the tape when it becomes full of leaves. Then use these finished projects as a unique bulletin board border!

Colleen Zeoli, Bright Start—Centralia School District, Anaheim, CA

POTATO PLAY

Pour the contents of a large box of instant mashed potato flakes into a tub. Then add warm water to the mixture until the product reaches the consistency of whipped potatoes. Place the tub in your sensory center along with potato mashers, ice cream scoops, and stirring spoons. Invite youngsters to the center to explore the unique texture of this popular Thanksgiving food.

Busy Hands

Seasonal Explorations for Little Hands

Lions, lambs, and shimmering gold! Your little ones are sure to have a blast with this collection of fun fine-motor activities!

ideas contributed by Tricia Brown, Brown's Academy for Boys Homeschool
Bowling Green, KY

LION AND LAMB

Place supersize lion and lamb head patterns at a table along with a supply of cotton balls, yellow tissue paper squares, and glue. Youngsters crumple the tissue paper squares, dip them in glue, and press them around the lion's face so they resemble the lion's mane. Then they dip cotton balls in glue and press them around the lamb's face so the cotton balls resemble wool. When the glue is dry, cut out the patterns. Then display the projects above fringed green construction paper so it appears as though the animals are peeking through tall grass.

SIFTING FOR GOLD

Fill a container with brown rice. Hide some gold nuggets (medium-size gold-painted stones) in the rice. Then provide access to a black plastic cauldron, such as the kind you can find at Halloween, and a strainer with holes large enough for the rice to pass through. A youngster uses the strainer to remove the gold from the rice; then he places the gold nuggets in the pot.

Colorful Kite

Attach a length of white paper to a table and draw an over-size kite on it. Invite two students at a time to use eyedroppers to drip tinted water on the kite. Then have each child blow air through a straw to move the drops around. After each child has had an opportunity to add to the project, cut out the kite and display it on a wall with a string and crepe paper streamers.

Lincoln's Log Cabin

Place graham cracker squares at a table along with a container of whipped cream cheese, a bowl of pretzel sticks, waxed paper, and plastic knives. A child visits the center, spreads cream cheese on a cracker half and places it on a piece of waxed paper. She presses pretzel sticks into the cream cheese so they resemble logs. Then she nibbles on her log cabin. What a fun way to recognize Presidents' Day!

Hearts Divided

Cut in half several same-size laminated heart shapes made from a variety of materials—such as a newspaper, magazines, scrapbook paper, paper towels, and wallpaper samples—and place them in a basket. A youngster places heart halves together to see how many different designs he can make. If desired, have the child glue his hearts to a sheet of paper to make a unique piece of artwork.

Busy Hands

Seasonal Explorations for Little Hands

Bees, caterpillars, planting, and more! Youngsters are sure to have a great time with this collection of fun spring explorations!

ideas contributed by Tricia Brown, Brown's Academy for Boys Homeschool
Bowling Green, KY

Honeycomb Hive

Place an oversize tagboard beehive drawing at a table along with a bowl of Honeycomb cereal, glue, a yellow stamp pad, and a black marker. Each youngster, in turn, glues pieces of cereal to the beehive outline. Then she makes yellow fingerprint bees around the hive. Finally, she uses the marker to draw details on each bee. When each child has had an opportunity to visit the center, display the finished hive.

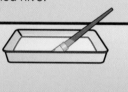

Fluffy Caterpillars

Cut out an oversize leaf shape and place it on the floor in a traffic-free area. Place a container of pom-poms in assorted sizes and colors next to the leaf. A child arranges the pom-poms on the leaf to make caterpillars in a variety of unique sizes and color combinations.

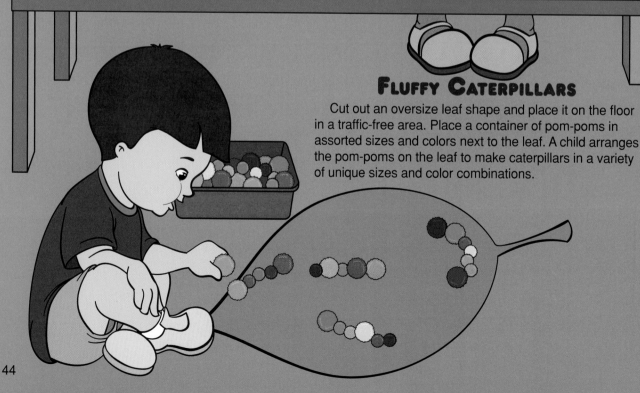

44

SPRING SHOWERS

A youngster draws a spring scene on a sheet of paper. Then she dips a plastic dish scrubber in blue tempera paint and drags the scrubber down the paper to make raindrops. Finally, she glues cotton balls to the top of her picture to make clouds.

PRESCHOOL PLANTERS

This idea is just perfect for little gardeners! Fill a large plastic garden planter or tub with potting soil. Provide a small plastic shovel and rake, craft foam seed cutouts, plastic flowers, gardening gloves, and a plastic watering can. A youngster uses the supplies for pretend planting.

BUG EXPEDITION

Hide several plastic bugs around your classroom. Provide a bug box, a magnifying glass, and a pair of tweezers. A child uses the magnifying glass to search around the room for the bugs. When she finds a bug, she picks it up with the tweezers and puts it in the bug box. What a fun way to collect bugs!

Busy Hands

Seasonal Explorations for Little Hands

Help youngsters kick off the summer season with these fine-motor activities!

ideas contributed by Janet Boyce, Cokato, MN

SANDCASTLES

Youngsters don't have to be at the beach to build sandcastles! Mix sand into a batch of light brown or white play dough. Place the play dough, along with plastic knives and ice cube trays, at a table. A child presses play dough into each section of an ice cube tray; then he gently removes the play dough using a plastic knife. He uses the resulting play dough cubes to build a sandcastle.

RACKET WEAVING

Tie a jumbo wooden bead to the end of each of several laces and place them in a container. Then provide access to a tennis or badminton racket. A youngster holds a lace by the end opposite the bead and then weaves it through the spaces between the racket strings. The wooden bead keeps the lace from slipping through the strings.

CIRCLE TIME

Circle Time

Exercise Photos

Youngsters get moving with this idea! To prepare, take pictures of your preschoolers performing a few simple exercises, such as toe touches and knee bends. Mount the pictures on index cards and store them in a bag. Invite a volunteer to pick a card from the bag and name the exercise shown on the card. Have him choose the number of repetitions to be done and then lead the group in some heart-healthy exercise!

Renee Bakken, Rochester Head Start, Rochester, MN

It's applesauce!

The Mystery Box

Before little ones arrive for the day, place a theme-related object or picture in a special mystery box. Once youngsters have arrived and are gathered in a group, engage their critical-thinking skills with a clue to help them discover what the item is. Continue prompting students with additional clues until the group determines what is inside the box. Then invite a volunteer to take the item out of the box for all to see. Repeat the process throughout the week by placing a new theme-related item in the mystery box each day.

Sueanne Deitering, Emmetsburg West Elementary
Emmetsburg, IA

Mystery Box

Body Part Bingo

Little ones are all winners when they play this fun-filled group game! In advance, prepare a set of cards, each labeled with a different body part. Give each child the same number of dot stickers as there are cards. To begin, have a child choose a card and name the corresponding body part; then have each youngster place one sticker on the body part that was called. Continue in this manner until all of the cards and stickers have been used and then have everyone in the group shout, "Bingo!"

Mischelle Fickessen, Jacinto City Elementary, Houston, TX

Stomp, stomp!

Who's Got the Rhythm?

Brainstorm with students the many ways they can move their bodies. Next, invite a volunteer to show the group an action she would like to do. Then lead the class in reciting the chant shown, substituting the child's name and the action in the final line. Continue in the same way until each child has had a turn.

Who's got the rhythm? Yeah! Yeah!
[Sarah] has the rhythm! [Stomp, stomp]!

Erin McGinness, Great New Beginnings, Newark, DE

Circle Time

The spoon!

Guess the Item

In advance, place a variety of items in a pocket chart. Secretly choose an item and then give a clue to help the class determine what the item is. Say, "I see something that [you eat with]." Then invite a volunteer to guess what the item is. Give additional clues if needed. Once the correct response is given, repeat the process with the remaining items.

Lisa Bishop
Elizabeth Wilhelm Elementary
North Las Vegas, NV

Clip and Pass

Youngsters get a real fine-motor workout with this activity! Bring to the circle an item that can easily be held with a spring-style clothespin. Give each child a clothespin and have him practice opening and closing it. Then clip your clothespin onto the item and pass it to the child next to you. Encourage each child, in turn, to use his clothespin to take the item and pass it to the child next to him. Continue until the item makes it all the way around the circle!

Heather J. Kelley, D. S. Perkins Elementary, Sulphur, LA

Safe, Safe, Fire!

To begin, choose a volunteer to pretend to be the firefighter. Have her walk around the circle and say, "Safe" each time she taps a different child on the shoulder; finally, she taps a child and says, "Fire." The firefighter returns to her seat, and the last child tapped goes to the middle of the circle and demonstrates how to stop, drop, and roll. The demonstrator then becomes the firefighter, and play continues in the same way.

Erica Crowder, Laurelville Head Start
Laurelville, OH

Picture Poem

In advance, make bat, hat, cat, and rat picture cards. Attach the cards to a wall in the order shown. Then recite the poem with your youngsters, pointing to each card to help youngsters supply the rhyming words.

I'm a brown bat; I'm a brown bat.
What rhymes with *bat? Hat!*
I'm a monster's hat; I'm a monster's hat.
What rhymes with *hat? Cat!*
I'm a black cat; I'm a black cat.
What rhymes with *cat? Rat!*
I'm a squeaky rat; I'm a squeaky rat,
And that is that!

Bonnie C. Krum
St. Matthew's Early Education Center
Bowie, MD

Circle Time

Circle!

Musical Shapes

Youngsters develop shape awareness with this engaging idea! Cut several supersize shapes from poster board; then laminate the shapes for durability. Scatter the shapes on the floor in your circle-time area. Play a recording of lively music and encourage little ones to dance. When you stop the music, call out a shape and have each child place a foot on the shape that was called. To aid little learners in finding the correct shape, hold up a small cutout identical to the large one that was called.

Nancy Barry, Barrypatch Child Care and Preschool
Greene, ME

My apple is green!

Let's Go Apple Picking!

In advance, make a class supply of red, yellow, and green construction paper apples and then use Sticky-Tac to post them around the classroom. Obtain a basket. Have each of several children find one apple to bring back to the circle. In turn, have each student identify the color of her apple and place her apple in the basket. Then send another small group of youngsters apple picking! For a variation later in the school year, add letters or numbers to the apples.

Debbie Dempsey, Chesterbrook Academy, Charlotte, NC

The Letter Patch

Program pumpkin cutouts with different letters. Have youngsters stand in a circle; then place a pumpkin on the floor in front of each child. Lead students in singing the song shown as youngsters walk around the circle of pumpkins. When the song ends, have each student stop in front of a pumpkin. Name a letter and prompt the children with matching letters to hold the pumpkins in the air. After confirming that each letter is correct, youngsters place the pumpkins back on the floor.

(sung to the tune of "Pawpaw Patch")

Where, oh, where can we find letters?
Where, oh, where can we find letters?
Where, oh, where can we find letters?
Way down yonder in the pumpkin patch!

Mary Robles, Portland, OR

Colorful Feathers

In advance, cut out a construction paper turkey body and feathers in different colors. Review the names of the colors with the class and then place the feathers on the turkey. Have students close their eyes. Then remove a feather and place it out of sight. Cue the children to open their eyes and name the color of the feather that is missing. After the color of the missing feather has been confirmed, place the feather back on the turkey. Continue in the same way as time allows.

Keely Peasner, Liberty Ridge Head Start
Bonney Lake, WA

The green feather is missing!

Circle Time

Indoor Snowstorm!

Little ones identify numbers with this fun idea! Label a class supply of snowflake cutouts with numbers. Obtain a white bedsheet. To begin, instruct each child to hold on to the edge of the sheet while you place the snowflakes in the center. Next, help students shake the sheet vigorously until each snowflake falls to the ground. Have each student pick up one snowflake and identify the number. If desired, place the snowflakes back on the sheet and get ready for another snowstorm!

Suzanne Maxymuk, Evergreen Avenue School, Woodbury, NJ, and
  Jen Wilson and Becky Seaman, Wonder Years Child Care,
  Jersey Shore, PA

Five!

Musical Drop

With this game, youngsters have all the fun of musical chairs without the chairs! Play some lively music and have students dance around in a circle. When you stop the music, youngsters see how fast they can drop to the floor and sit quietly with their legs crossed. After several moments of silence, have students stand up and play another round.

Mary Fowler, Weston County Children Center, Upton, WY

Lost Mittens

Make two white construction paper mittens for each student. (See page 193 for mitten patterns.) Then hide the mittens around your classroom. Lead youngsters in reciting the nursery rhyme "The Three Little Kittens." Then have each youngster pretend to be a kitten looking for its lost mittens. After each child finds two mittens, invite him to color them as desired. Finally, use a hole puncher to make a hole in the top of each mitten and tie the pair together with a length of yarn.

MaryJo Griese
W. J. Kossman School
Long Valley, NJ

Rhyme-Time Snowman

Enlarge a copy of the rhyming cards on page 65. Then cut out the cards and glue each one to a different white circle cutout. Decorate a separate white circle cutout so it resembles a snowman's head. Place the head on the floor along with the prepared circles. Then gather youngsters around the cutouts. Invite a volunteer to choose a circle, name the picture, and then find its matching picture rhyme. Next, have her place the circles under the snowman's head so they resemble the middle and the bottom of the body. Lead the class in the chant shown. Then remove the circles and repeat the process.

Words that rhyme are fun, you see.
Here's a snowman: one, two, three!

Dawn Seigel
Evergreen Avenue School
Woodbury, NJ

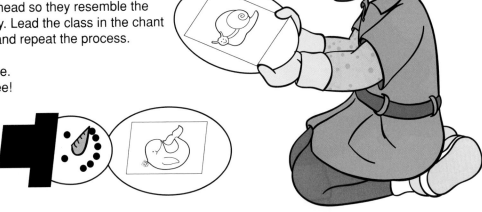

Circle Time

Pancake Shuffle

Little ones practice early subtraction skills with this twist on a familiar rhyme! Cut out five brown construction paper pancake shapes. Place each pancake on a separate paper plate. Obtain an empty pancake syrup bottle. To begin, pretend to squirt syrup over each pancake as youngsters count the number of pancakes aloud. Then guide students in reciting the rhyme shown, inserting a child's name and prompting him to take a pancake when indicated. Continue in the same manner until all of the pancakes are gone.

Down around the corner at the pancake shop,
There were five little pancakes with syrup on top.
Along came [child's name], all alone,
Who ate one pancake and then went home.

Nancy Foss, Wee Care Preschool, Galion, OH

Peck a Letter

Program several craft foam seed cutouts with different letters. Obtain a bird puppet or stuffed bird toy. To begin, scatter the birdseed faceup on the floor. Then invite a student to "fly" the bird around the circle as you recite the chant shown. After you make the letter sound, the child gently swoops the bird to the floor and uses it to peck the seed with the corresponding letter. Then have her pass the bird to a classmate. Continue as time allows.

Little birdie, fly to the ground
And peck the letter that makes the sound [/s/].

Donna Brock
High Desert Montessori Child Care Center
Hesperia, CA

58

Happy St. Patrick's Day!

Where's the Leprechaun?

In advance, attach a supply of shamrocks (patterns on page 94) to a length of green bulletin board paper so each one can be lifted like a flap. Mount the field of shamrocks to a wall. To play, have little ones close their eyes while you hide a leprechaun cutout under a shamrock using Sticky-Tac. Instruct youngsters to open their eyes; then lead the class in reciting the chant shown. Invite students to take turns lifting the shamrocks. When the leprechaun is found, have children say, "Happy St. Patrick's Day!"

Leprechaun, leprechaun,
Out of view,
We'll keep looking
Till we find you!

Rebecca Perruquet, Danville Elementary, Danville, PA

I spy a shadow!

Groundhog's Shadow

In advance, enlarge the groundhog pattern on page 224 and make a copy. Then cut out the pattern and trace it on black construction paper to make a shadow. Cut out the shadow and hide it in your classroom. At circle time, show the groundhog cutout to students. Then tell youngsters that the groundhog's shadow is hidden somewhere in the classroom. Have students look for the shadow and instruct them to call out, "I spy a shadow!" when it is found.

Keely Peasner
Liberty Ridge Head Start
Bonney Lake, WA

Circle Time

Plant Parts

In advance, make felt plant parts as shown. To begin, introduce youngsters to each plant part and its name as you build the plant on your flannelboard. Next, invite a volunteer to point to each plant part as you lead the class in singing the song below. Then remove the pieces from the flannelboard. Invite another volunteer to rebuild the plant; then lead the group in repeating the song. Continue in the same manner as time allows.

(sung to the tune of "Are You Sleeping?")

Leaves and flowers, roots and stem
Are the parts of a plant.
Let's name them again.
Let's name them again.
Leaves and flowers, roots and stem.

Michelle Freed, Peru State College, Peru, NE

It's Raining Numbers!

Program a class supply of light blue raindrop cutouts with numbers from 1 to 10. Place an open umbrella upside down on the floor and place the raindrops inside. Lead youngsters in singing a rain-related song, such as "Rain, Rain, Go Away." When the song ends, hold the umbrella upright, creating a shower of raindrops! Then instruct each child to pick up a raindrop and identify the number. After checking for accuracy, have students place the raindrops back in the umbrella and get ready for another rain shower!

Leslie Boyett
Asbury Ark Academy
Bossier City, LA

Car!

Cassie Caterpillar

To prepare for this activity, make a caterpillar drawing similar to the one shown. Cut out a copy of the cards on page 66 and place the cards facedown on the floor. To begin, invite a volunteer to pick a card and name the picture. If the word begins with the hard /c/ sound, have the child place the card on the caterpillar. If it does not, have him put the card aside. Continue in the same manner until all of the cards have been turned over.

Carolyn Bertog
Chavez Learning Station
Kenosha, WI

One, two, three...

Puddle Jumpers

Place a blue bedsheet or blanket (puddle) on the floor. Label several cloud cutouts with different numbers. To begin, lead students in singing the song shown as they walk around the outside of the puddle. When the song ends, hold up a cloud and have students identify the number. Then prompt youngsters to step on the puddle and jump the appropriate number of times.

(sung to the tune of "Did You Ever See a Lassie?")

Oh, it's fun to jump in puddles, in puddles, in puddles.
Oh, it's fun to jump in puddles on gray, rainy days.
I splish splash and splish splash
And splish splash and splish splash.
Oh, it's fun to jump in puddles on gray, rainy days.

Alicia Houser, Discovery Junction, Campbelltown, PA

61

Circle Time

Mystery Food

Collect familiar food labels, wrappers, or box panels. Cut out the name of the item; then cut the remainder of each label into several puzzle pieces. Store each puzzle in a separate resealable plastic bag. To begin, display a food name and ask students if they can identify it. Then give youngsters a clue by adding a puzzle piece to the name. Continue in the same manner until the name of the food has been identified.

Staci Peterson
Voyager Elementary
Alexandria, MN

That says Toastios!

Toastios

I rule the pool!

Rule the Pool

Little ones will dive right into this activity! To begin, place on the floor a blue blanket (or blue paper) so it resembles a pool. Invite five youngsters to pretend they are swimming in the pool. Then lead the remaining group in singing the song shown, encouraging the child named to leap out of the pool and join the group. Repeat the verse three more times, substituting a different child's name each time, until there is one child left. Then prompt him to say, "I rule the pool!"

(sung to the tune of "Ten in a Bed")

There were [five] in the pool
And the little one said, "Roll over, roll over."
So they all rolled over and
   [Christian] leaped out!

Rebecca Perruquet, Here We Grow Preschool
Danville, PA

Splendid Sprinkles

In advance, prepare a supersize ice cream cone cutout and attach several numbered scoop cutouts to the cone. Place the ice cream cone on your floor. Gather a container of small multicolored pom-poms (sprinkles) and a large spoon. Gather youngsters around the ice cream cone. Announce a number and ask a child to take a spoonful of sprinkles and place them on the ice cream scoop labeled with that number. Continue in the same way until all youngsters have added sprinkles to the scoops.

Kristina Wisner, Forest Christian Child Care Center
Upperco, MD

Doggie, Doggie

To prepare for this game, label a class supply of dog-bone cutouts with different letters. Invite a volunteer to pretend to be a napping dog. Give each remaining child in the group a dog bone. To wake the doggie, chant, "Doggie, where's the bone with the *B?* Someone has it, but it isn't me!" The doggie picks one of the children, who then holds up her bone and identifies the letter. Play continues until the doggie picks the child with the correct bone; then she becomes the doggie. When she is "asleep," have students exchange bones with classmates. Then play another round!

Leigh Ann Peter, Buttonwood Preschool, Lumberton, NJ

They all fit!

Is There Room?

Youngsters reinforce counting skills and spatial awareness with this activity! Obtain a plastic hoop along with a collection of 20 items, such as toy cars. Ask little ones to predict if they think all the items will fit inside the hoop. Then have youngsters count aloud as you place each item from the collection in the hoop. Compare the outcome with student predictions. Then invite each child to name a collection of objects that would not fit inside the hoop, such as 20 elephants!

Maryann Bennett
Tutor Time, Scottsdale, AZ

Wiggly Worm

Little ones reinforce basic concepts and get exercise with this fun idea! Program cards with desired symbols, such as shapes or numbers. Include in the card set several cards programmed with a cute wiggly worm. Place the cards in a decorative bag. Then invite a child to choose a card. The child holds up the card, and the remaining students identify the shape. If a wiggly worm card is revealed, have the group stand up and wiggle! Continue until each child has had a turn to hold up a card.

Megan Grimm, Delaware Area Career Center Preschool
Delaware, OH

TEC41034   TEC41034   TEC41034   TEC41034

TEC41034   TEC41034   TEC41034   TEC41034

Penguin Pattern
Use with "Slippery Sledding" on page 57.

TEC41034

Beginning Sounds Picture Cards
Use with "Cassie Caterpillar" on page 61.

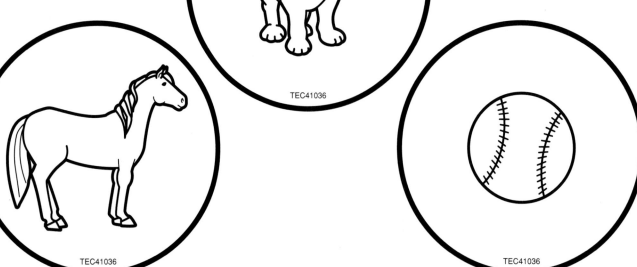

TEC41036

TEC41036

TEC41036

TEC41036

TEC41036

TEC41036

TEC41036

TEC41036

66

KIDS IN THE KITCHEN

KIDS IN THE KITCHEN

Have little ones relive fond memories of summer with this adorable swimming pool snack! What a perfectly pleasing treat for the beginning of the school year!

To prepare for the snack:
- Collect the necessary ingredients, utensils, and supplies using the lists on the recipe card below.
- Photocopy the step-by-step recipe cards on page 69.
- Color the cards; then cut them out and display them in your snack area.
- Follow the teacher preparation guidelines for the snack.

Swimming Pool Snack

Ingredients for one:
cake-style dessert shell
vanilla pudding, tinted blue
piece of O-shaped cereal
   (inner tube)

Utensils and supplies:
large plastic bowl
small plastic bowl
serving spoon
disposable plate for each child
plastic spoon for each child

Teacher preparation:
   Place the pudding in the large bowl and the cereal in the small bowl. Put the serving spoon near the pudding. Arrange the ingredients, utensils, and supplies near the step-by-step recipe cards.

Michele Fein and Helene Kuperberg
Discovery Preschool
Boca Raton, FL

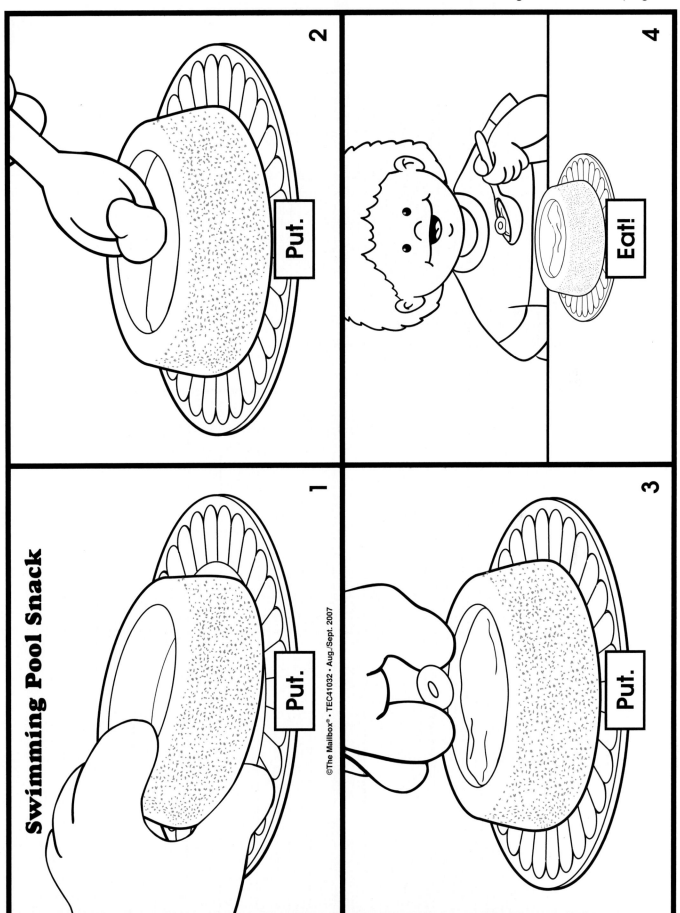

2

Put.

4

Eat!

Swimming Pool Snack

1

Put.

3

Put.

This fun little snack is a perfect accompaniment to a read-aloud of *The Hat* by Jan Brett. See pages 166 and 167 for activities to go with this engaging story.

To prepare for the snack:

- Collect the necessary ingredients and utensils using the lists on the recipe card below.
- Photocopy the step-by-step recipe cards on page 71.
- Cut out the cards and display them in your snack area.
- Follow the teacher preparation guidelines for the snack.

Happy Hedgehog

Ingredients for one:
portion of a banana (see below)
crushed Honey Nut Chex cereal
3 M&M's Minis chocolate candies

Utensils and supplies:
disposable plate for each child
napkin for each child
plastic fork for each child

Teacher preparation:
Slice a banana in half lengthwise; then slice the pieces in half again widthwise to make four sections. Arrange the ingredients and supplies near the step-by-step recipe cards.

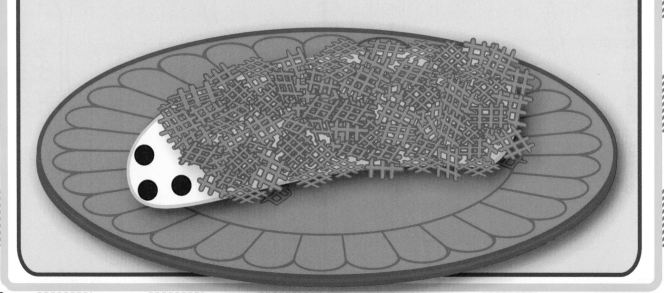

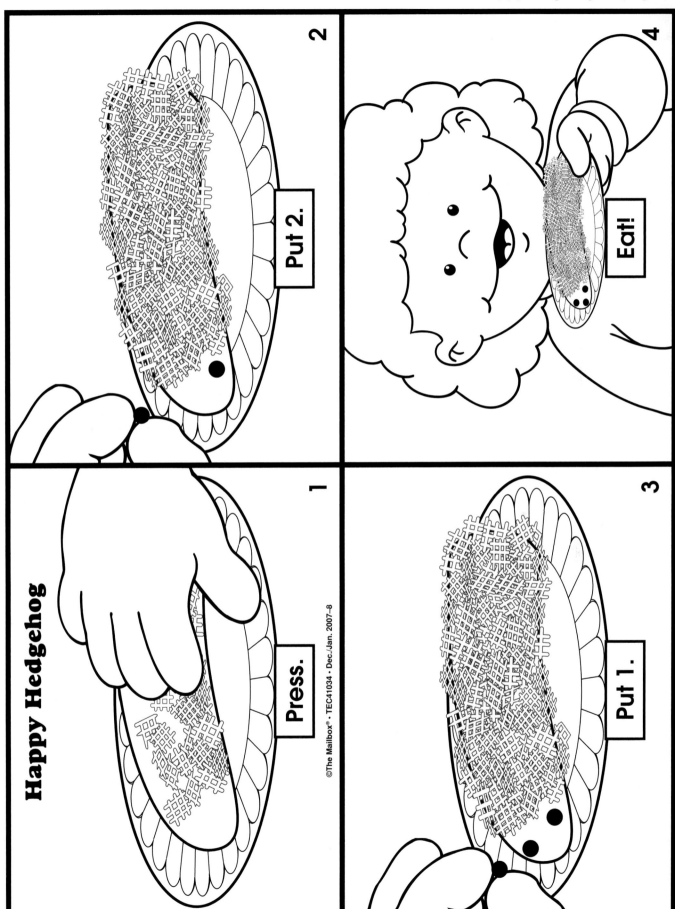

Happy Hedgehog

Press.

Put 2.

Put 1.

Eat!

KIDS IN THE KITCHEN

Serve up some pleasing pies with this fun Presidents' Day recipe. You may wish to share the myth of George Washington and the cherry tree with your little ones before they make their snacks.

To prepare for the snack:
- Collect the necessary ingredients and utensils using the lists on the recipe card below.
- Photocopy the step-by-step recipe cards on page 73.
- Color the cards; then cut them out and display them in the snack area.
- Follow the teacher preparation guidelines for the snack.

President's Pie

Ingredients for one:
2 chocolate wafer cookies
cherry pie filling
whipped topping

Utensils and supplies:
plastic container
disposable cup for each child
plastic spoon for each child
resealable plastic bag for each child
small ice cream scoop
toothpick flag for each child (optional)

Teacher preparation:
Place the cherry pie filling in the plastic container and put the ice cream scoop in the pie filling. Arrange the ingredients, utensils, and supplies near the step-by-step recipe cards.

Janet Boyce
Cokato, MN

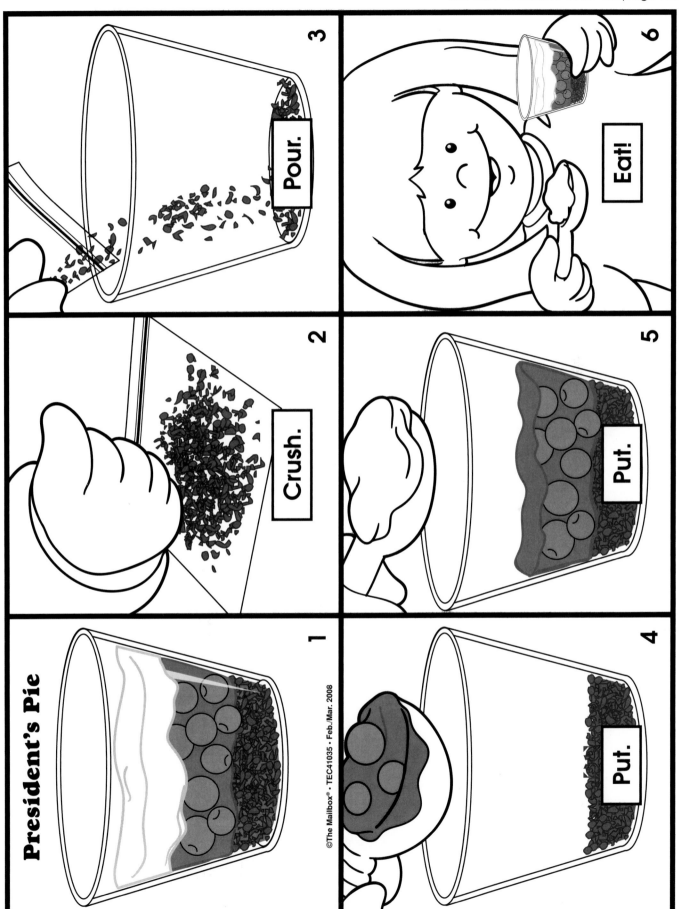

President's Pie

3 Pour.

2 Crush.

1

6 Eat!

5 Put.

4 Put.

This tasty snack resembles a popular summer-time treat!

To prepare for the snack:
- Collect the necessary ingredients and utensils using the lists on the recipe card below.
- Photocopy the step-by-step recipe cards on page 75.
- Color the cards; then cut them out and display them in the snack area.
- Follow the teacher preparation guidelines for the snack.

A Slice of Watermelon

Ingredients for one:
half of a soft sugar cookie
red-tinted frosting
mini chocolate chips

Utensils and supplies:
disposable plate for each child
napkin for each child
plastic knife

Teacher preparation:
Arrange the ingredients, utensils, and supplies near the step-by-step recipe cards.

Nancy Foss
Wee Care Day Care
Galion, OH

Jennie Jensen
North Cedar Elementary
Lowden, IA

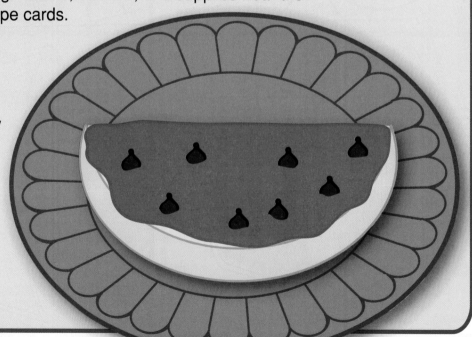

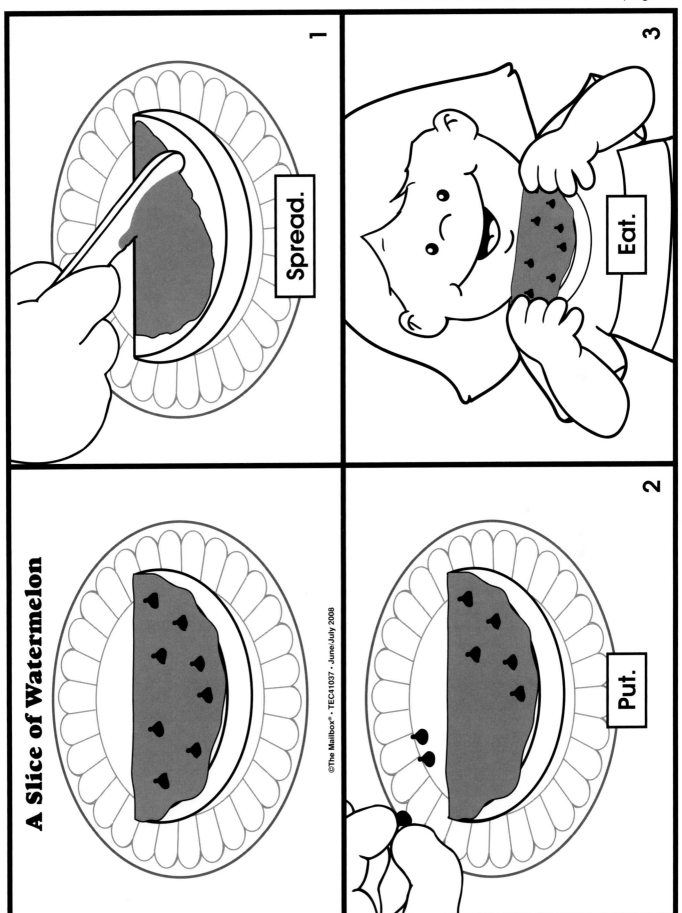

1

Spread.

3

Eat.

A Slice of Watermelon

2

Put.

©The Mailbox® • TEC41037 • June/July 2008

This tasty butterfly sandwich is the perfect springtime snack.

To prepare for this snack:
- Collect the necessary ingredients and utensils using the lists on the recipe card below. If desired, use the parent letter on page 78 to help obtain supplies.
- Photocopy the step-by-step recipe cards on page 77.
- Color the cards; then cut them out and display them in the snack area.
- Follow the teacher preparation guidelines for the snack.

Beautiful Butterfly

Ingredients for one:
slice of bread
vegetable cream cheese
cucumber stick

Utensils and supplies:
disposable plate for each child
plastic knife for each child

Teacher preparation:
Arrange the ingredients and supplies near the step-by-step recipe cards.

Melissa Rose
Early Childhood Alliance
Fort Wayne, IN

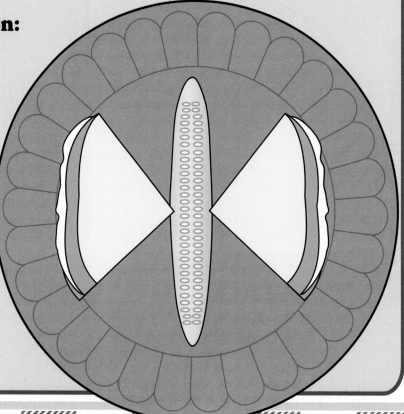

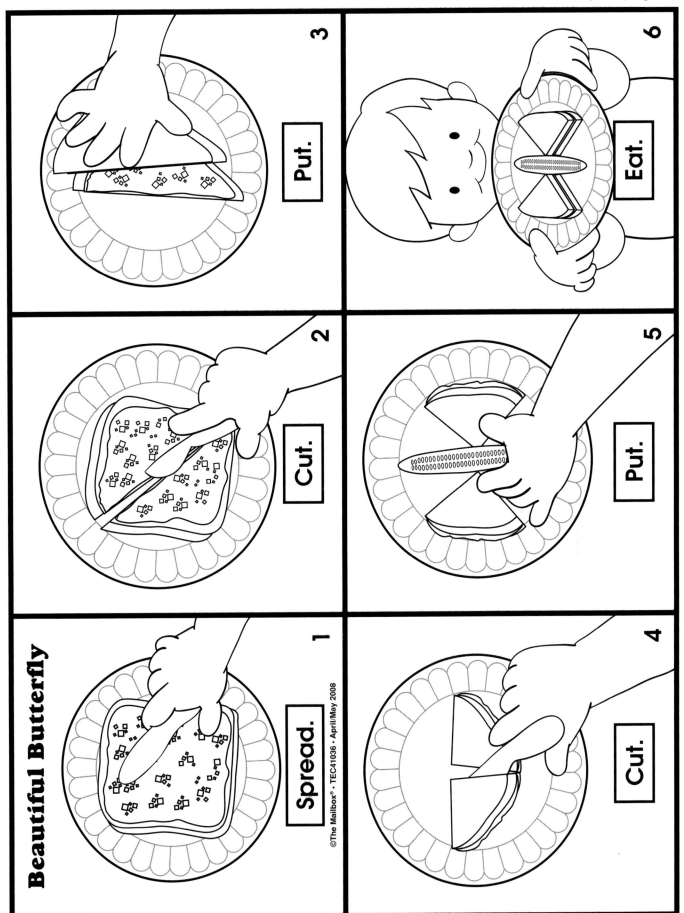

Beautiful Butterfly

1 — Spread.

2 — Cut.

3 — Put.

4 — Cut.

5 — Put.

6 — Eat.

©The Mailbox® • TEC41036 • April/May 2008

Parent Notes
Use with "Beautiful Butterfly" on page 76.

Dear Parent,
We are making a Beautiful Butterfly Snack soon. We would be grateful if you could help by providing the following ingredient(s):

_____

_____

_____

We need the ingredient(s) listed above by _____.
date
Please let me know if you are able to send the ingredient(s).
Thank you,

_____
teacher

☐ Yes, I am able to send the ingredient(s).
☐ No, I am unable to send the ingredient(s) this time.

_____
parent signature

Dear Parent,
We are making a Beautiful Butterfly Snack soon. We would be grateful if you could help by providing the following ingredient(s):

_____

_____

_____

We need the ingredient(s) listed above by _____.
date
Please let me know if you are able to send the ingredient(s).
Thank you,

_____
teacher

☐ Yes, I am able to send the ingredient(s).
☐ No, I am unable to send the ingredient(s) this time.

_____
parent signature

LEARNING CENTERS

Learning Centers

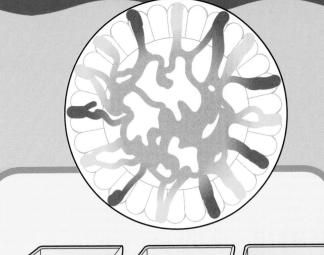

Drip and Mix
Art Center

Use food coloring to tint each of three containers of water a different primary color. Place the containers at a table along with paper plates and eyedroppers. A child uses the eyedroppers to drip two or three different colors of tinted water along the edges of her plate. She then watches the colors mix on her plate to make a simple yet unique masterpiece.

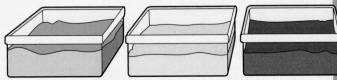

Janet Boyce
Cokato, MN

Glove Squeeze
Sensory Center

Gather several latex-free rubber gloves; then fill each glove with a different substance. You might want to consider using cornstarch, rice, salt, shaving cream, or aquarium gravel. (Double the gloves for increased durability.) Then seal each glove with a rubber band. Place the gloves at a center and allow students to squeeze them to feel the different textures.

Jayne Jaskolski
Twenty-First Street School
Milwaukee, WI

Grocery Lists
Literacy Center

Cut out pictures from grocery store circulars and attach each one to a paper strip. Write the name of each item next to its picture. Then laminate the strips for durability. Also laminate a supply of blank strips. Place the strips at a center and provide access to wipe-off markers. Youngsters visit the center and use the markers to trace the words or to write items of their choosing on the blank strips.

Christine Wirt
Tiny Tot Station
Elk Grove, CA

Learning Centers

Photo Puzzles
Flannelboard Center

Take several photographs of your youngsters throughout the day and then enlarge the photos. Glue each photo to a piece of felt. When the glue is dry, puzzle-cut the photos and then place each puzzle in a separate resealable plastic bag. Place the bags near your flannelboard. A youngster chooses a puzzle and removes the pieces from the bag. Then she attaches the pieces to the flannelboard to complete the photo. For a variation on this activity, see "Family Connection" on page 180.

Ellen Conti
Our Lady of the Assumption Nursery School
Copiague, NY

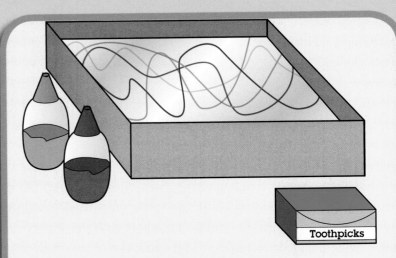

Gelatin Drawing
Science Center

In advance, make a batch of clear unflavored gelatin in a large shallow pan. When the gelatin has solidified, place it at a center along with toothpicks with rounded ends and food coloring. Have a youngster visit the center and place a couple of drops of food coloring on the gelatin. Then have him use a pincer grasp to hold a toothpick and drag it through the food coloring and across the gelatin. The food coloring will follow the toothpick and make lines in the gelatin. Have him repeat the process several times.

Gena M. Groh
Trapper School
Nuiqsut, AK

Glorious Gumballs
Math Center

Youngsters practice drawing circles with this idea! Make a simple gumball machine pattern and then copy it to make a class supply. Place the patterns at a table along with crayons and a circle cutout. A youngster visits the center and traces the circle with her finger, identifying the name of the shape as she traces. Then she draws a variety of circles on her pattern to make gumballs. Finally, she colors the gumballs and the gumball machine.

Rebekah Anderson
South Heights, Sapulpa, OK

Learning Centers

Pleasing Placemats
Craft Center

Gather magazines and grocery store circulars and place them at a table along with glue sticks and 12" x 18" sheets of construction paper programmed as shown. (If desired, cover the table with a Thanksgiving-related vinyl tablecloth.) A youngster cuts out pictures of favorite foods and glues them to his paper to make a Thanksgiving placemat. When each child has had an opportunity to visit the center, laminate the finished placemats for durability.

Janet Boyce
Cokato, MN

Prickly Porcupines
Fine-Motor Area

Little ones strengthen fine-motor skills on this porcupine hunt! Obtain a supply of porcupine balls. Then add the balls to your sensory table along with a supply of plastic fall-colored leaves. Set a container and a pair of tongs nearby. A child uses the tongs to pick up a porcupine and place it in the container. She continues in the same way with the remaining porcupines.

Vicki Brant
Ravenna, OH

Crowing for Corn
Math Center

Color and cut out two copies of the crow pattern on page 92. Also make a supply of yellow construction paper corn kernels. Place the crows, the corn, and a jumbo die in your math center. Two children visit the center, and each child takes a crow. One youngster rolls the die and places the corresponding number of kernels on his crow. His partner repeats the process. After the youngsters compare the amounts, they play another round!

Angie Kutzer
Garret Elementary
Mebane, NC

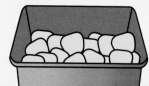

Delectable Desserts
Play Dough Center

To prepare, combine the ingredients shown in a large saucepan. Then cook the mixture over low heat until it becomes the consistency of play dough. After the dough has cooled, place it in a center along with utensils, such as rolling pins, plastic butter knives, cookie cutters, pie tins, and plates. A youngster uses the dough and utensils to make pumpkin-scented treats.

Keely Peasner
Liberty Ridge Head Start
Bonney Lake, WA

Pumpkin Dough

Ingredients:
5 1/2 c. flour
2 c. salt
8 tsp. cream of tartar
3/4 c. vegetable oil
1 1/2 c. pumpkin spice
4 c. water
orange food coloring

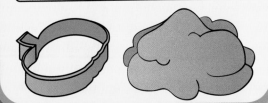

Hooray for Hay!
Block Center

In advance, wrap several lidded boxes with brown mailing paper or paper grocery bags. Enlist youngsters' help in painting the boxes yellow. Then add details to each box so that they resemble bales of hay. Place the hay in your block area, along with other fall-related items, such as child-size rakes and bushel baskets filled with plastic leaves. A child uses the props to engage in fall-related dramatic play.

Renee Brown
New Adventure Learning Center
Brevard, NC

A Leafy Letter
Literacy Center

Take little ones on a leaf-collecting walk to prepare for this cooperative letter-formation activity. After the leaves have been collected, tape a sheet of bulletin board paper to a table in your literacy center. Then draw an oversize letter *L* outline on the paper. Children name the letter and its sound and then glue leaves inside the outline.

Learning Centers

Wrap and Unwrap!
Fine-Motor Area

In advance, cut out pictures of gift items from magazines or store circulars and attach each one to a wooden block using clear packing tape. Place the blocks at a table, along with wrapping paper, scissors, and tape. A student visits the center and uses the supplies to wrap the pretend gifts. He may wish to exchange his gifts with those of a classmate. Then the students can unwrap the gifts.

Melissa Weimer
Stepanski Early Childhood Center
Waterford, MI

Snowball Toss
Gross-Motor Area

Gather a container and a supply of clean white socks. Roll each sock from the bottom up and then pull the cuff over the rolled-up portion so the sock resembles a snowball. Place the container, along with the snowballs, in an open area. A youngster visits the center and tosses each snowball into the container.

Melanie Hays
Crossgates Methodist Children's Center
Brandon, MS

Magnetic Snowpal
Dramatic Play

Obtain three large popcorn tins in graduated sizes. Paint each tin white and then drill two armholes in the medium-size tin. Hot-glue foam shapes to magnets to be used for facial features and other details. Place the tins and the shapes at a center, along with two sticks and a variety of winter accessories. A visiting youngster stacks the tins, inserts the sticks into the armholes, and then uses the shapes and winter wear to create a snowpal.

Cherie Rissman
Meredith Drive Preschool
Des Moines, IA

Calendar Match
Literacy Center

Old calendars will be put to good use with this idea! Cut pictures from an expired theme calendar, such as a dog calendar. Then cut out an equal set of corresponding shapes, such as bones. Pair the pictures and shapes and then label each pair with matching letters. Place the items at a center. A visiting student matches each picture with its corresponding shape.

Dorothy Stein
Christian Beginnings Preschool
Prince Frederick, MD

Menorah Mats
Math Center

Children practice counting with this Hanukkah-themed idea! In advance, obtain a supply of birthday candles and a large die. Color, cut out, and laminate two copies of the menorah pattern on page 93. Place the menorahs, the candles, and the die at a table. A pair of youngsters visits the center and each child takes a menorah. In turn, each student rolls the die, counts aloud the corresponding number of candles, and places them on his menorah. Play continues until each menorah is complete.

Susan Finklestein
Saint James School
Montgomery, AL

Salty Snow
Sensory Center

In advance, hot-glue cardboard rectangles to the front of toy pickup trucks to make snowplows. Fill your sensory table with salt. Place the snowplows in the table, along with plastic animals. Youngsters visit the center and use the snowplows to clear the way for the animals.

Karen Briley
Stephen F. Austin State University Early Childhood Lab
Nacogdoches, TX

Learning Centers

Valentine Halves
Puzzle Center

Little ones practice visual discrimination skills with this idea! Laminate several leftover valentines. Cut each valentine in half, using a different puzzle-cut for each card. Store the puzzles in a resealable plastic bag. A child visits the center and removes the pieces from the bag. Then she places the matching puzzle halves together to complete each valentine.

Lois Otten
Kingdom Kids Preschool
Sheboygan, WI

Counting the Gold
Math Center

In advance, spray-paint the entire surface of a muffin tin black. Drizzle glue around the top of each section of the tin and then sprinkle gold glitter on the glue so the sections resemble mini pots of gold. Use correction fluid to label each pot of gold with a different number. Place the pots at a center along with a supply of yellow craft foam circles (coins). A visiting child identifies the number in one of the pots and then places the corresponding number of coins in the pot. He continues in the same way with the remaining pots of gold.

Tanya Tschombor
Childtime Learning Center
Brea, CA

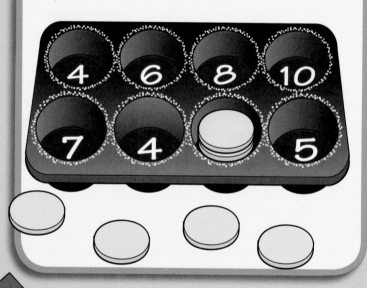

Hearts and Arrows
Literacy Center

To prepare, label each of several tagboard hearts with a different letter. Label an equal number of red triangle cutouts with the matching letters. Then attach the triangles to red clothespins so they resemble arrows. Place the hearts and the arrows at a center. A youngster visits the center and clips an arrow to the heart with the matching letter. She continues in the same manner with the remaining arrows.

Christine Joyce
Christine Joyce Child Care
Warwick, NY

Clover Picking
Sensory Center

In advance, cut out several green construction paper copies of the clover patterns on page 94. Add the cutouts to your sensory table along with a supply of green crinkle strips. Place two plastic pails nearby, labeled as shown. A child picks a cutout from the grass, identifies whether it's a three- or four-leaf clover, and places it in the corresponding pail.

Mary Robles
Milwaukie, OR

Bottles and Caps
Fine-Motor Area

Gather an assortment of clean plastic bottles with caps, along with a thick sheet of polystyrene foam. Cut each bottle in half and discard the bottom portion. Press the remaining bottle halves into the foam as shown. Place the foam in a center along with the bottle caps. A child chooses a cap and then screws the cap onto the corresponding bottle. Then he removes each cap for the next visiting child.

Melissa Bustamante
Melissa's Preschool
Buda, TX

Super Shamrocks
Art Center

In advance, obtain a green bell pepper with three lobes. Cut the pepper in half horizontally and remove the seeds. Then place the pepper halves at a table along with a shallow container of green paint. A child visiting the center presses a pepper half into the paint and then presses the pepper onto a sheet of white construction paper to create a shamrock. She repeats the process until a desired effect is achieved. Then she sprinkles glitter (leprechaun dust) over the wet paint.

Janet Boyce
Cokato, MN

Learning Centers

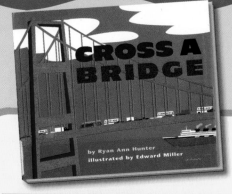

Beautiful Bridges
Block Center

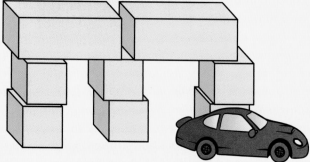

Youngsters develop motor skills with this bridge-building idea! Put in your block center books about bridges, photographs showing a variety of bridges, and toy cars and boats. A child visits the center and refers to the books and photographs to build a bridge of his own. Then he moves the cars over and boats under his bridge.

Lisa Addington
Chadwicks, NY

Showers Galore!
Games Center

Cut the centers from four craft foam cloud cutouts and hot-glue each cloud to a disposable cup as shown. Also cut out a supply of craft foam raindrops. Place the cloud cups, the raindrops, and a die at a table. Visiting youngsters each take a cloud cup. In turn, each student rolls the die, counts aloud the corresponding number of raindrops, and puts them in her cloud cup. When there are no raindrops left, each child pours the raindrops from her cloud cup onto the table as she chants, "It's raining! It's pouring!"

Lisa E. Desrosiers
Gates Lane School
Worcester, MA

Turtle Tubs
Literacy Center

Use masking tape to make the letter *T* on plastic tubs as shown. Place the labeled tubs in a center. A child traces the letter with his finger as he says its name. Then he places the tub on his back and crawls around on his hands and knees pretending to be a turtle!

Jen Wilson and Becky Seaman
Wonder Years Child Care
Jersey Shore, PA

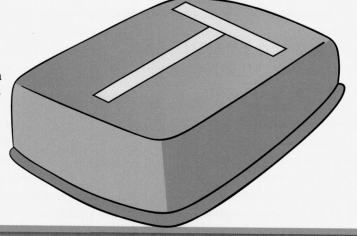

Duck Ponds
Math Center

Program pond cutouts with different shapes. Then label duck cutouts with shapes that correspond to the pond shapes. Place the ponds and the ducks at a center. A child places each duck on the appropriate pond.

Katharine Petitt
Lutheran Home Child Care
Wauwatosa, WI

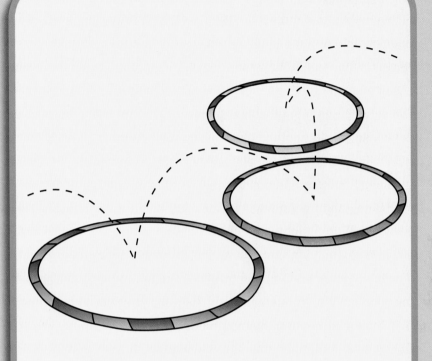

Little Leapers
Gross-Motor Area

Position several plastic hoops (lily pads) in a row on your floor. A youngster pretends to be a frog as he jumps from lily pad to lily pad chanting, "Ribbit, ribbit, ribbit!"

Cindy Wetzig
Bethany Lutheran Preschool
Fairview Heights, IL

Bunny Stampers
Art Center

In advance, prepare several bunny stampers by hot-gluing a block to a wooden clothespin as shown. Place the bunny stampers at a table along with shallow pans of tempera paint and construction paper. A child holds the stamper by the block, presses the clothespin in the paint, and makes prints on a sheet of paper. When the paint is dry, he uses a marker to make facial features on each bunny.

Karen Amatrudo
Madison, CT

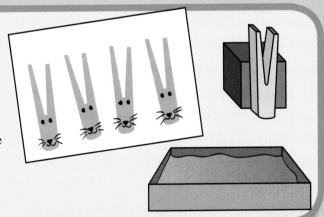

Terrific Tentacles
Fine-Motor Area

For each child, punch large holes along the edge of a paper plate half as shown. Place the plate halves at a center along with a supply of 12-inch lengths of yarn. A child visits the center and folds a length of yarn in half. She threads the looped end of the yarn through a hole. Then she pulls the loose ends of the yarn through the loop to create tentacles. She continues in the same manner with each remaining hole. Then she draws a face on her jellyfish.

Karen Eiben
The Learning House Preschool
La Salle, IL

Ants at the Picnic
Math Center

Label each of several picnic-related food cutouts with a different number. Attach the cutouts to a plastic tablecloth. Prepare each of an equal number of ant cutouts with a corresponding dot set. Place the tablecloth and the ants at a center. A visiting youngster identifies the number on a food cutout and then places the ant with the corresponding dot set by the food. He continues in the same way with the remaining food.

Erica Scholl
Cornerstone Head Start
Utica, NY

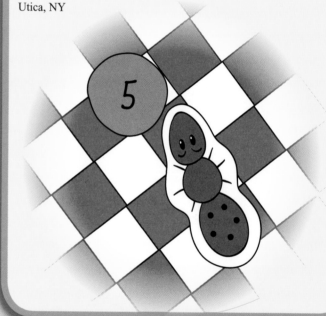

Fabulous Fireflies
Art Center

Youngsters create a cozy atmosphere with this cute idea! Place at a center black paper, brown paper scraps, orange tissue paper, glue, and glitter glue. A visiting child tears several brown paper strips (logs) and glues them to a sheet of black paper. Then she glues torn pieces of tissue paper above the logs so the paper resembles flames. Finally, she dabs glitter glue around the campfire to make fireflies.

Trystajill Harns
Lakeside Christian School
East Lansing, MI

Letter Rubbings
Literacy Center

Miscellaneous bulletin board letters will be put to good use with this idea! Simply tape several different letters to a table in a center. Provide a supply of light-colored paper and several unwrapped crayons. A youngster visits the center and names one of the letters. After he places a sheet of paper on top of the letter, he rubs the side of a crayon across the paper to reveal the letter underneath.

Brooke Beverly
Dudley Elementary School
Dudley, MA

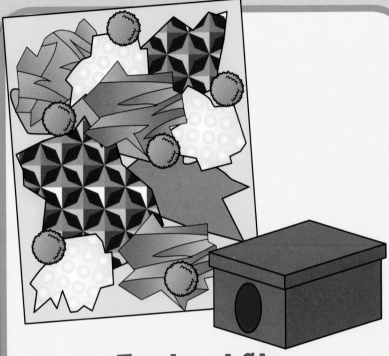

Touch and Glue
Sensory Center

Place a variety of collage items with different textures in a box with a hole cut in the side. Place the box at a center along with a sheet of poster board and glue. In turn, each visiting child reaches in the box and describes an item's texture. Then she removes the item from the box and glues it to the board. After the board is dry, hang it in your sensory area for further exploration.

Donna Foss
Middlebury, CT

Car Wash
Gross-Motor Area

In advance, tape lengths of blue crepe paper to both ends of a long table so it resembles a car wash. Put several large cars and trucks in the center. A child visits the center and chooses a vehicle. He enters one end of the makeshift car wash and crawls along, pushing his vehicle until he exits from the opposite end.

Andrea Henderson
Jefferson Brethren Preschool
Goshen, IN

Crow Pattern

Use with "Crowing for Corn" on page 82 and "The Friendly Scarecrow" on page 142.

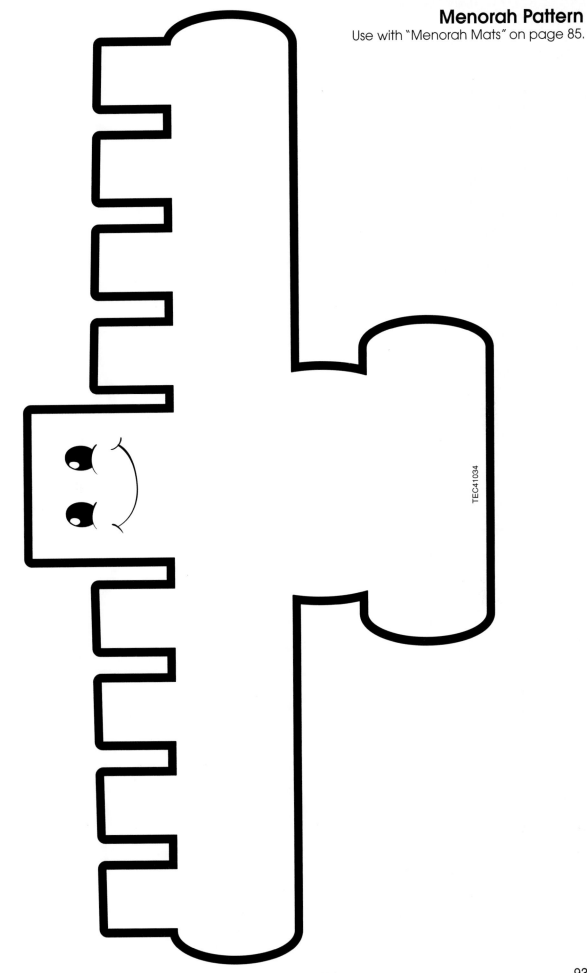

TEC41034

Three- and Four-Leaf Clover Patterns
Use with "Where's the Leprechaun?" on page 59 and "Clover Picking" on page 87.

TEC41035

TEC41035

TEC41035

TEC41035

MANAGEMENT TIPS & TIMESAVERS

Management Tips & Timesavers

The Snack Bag

Here's a simple snacktime organization system! Make a copy of a calendar for the upcoming month and label each school day with a child's name, repeating names as needed. Send home a copy of the calendar with each child along with any snacktime tips and directions. Decorate a plain canvas tote bag. Then send the tote home with the child who will provide the snacks for the next day. The bag makes a terrific snack reminder! *Stephanie Morrison, Wolf Creek Elementary, Broken Arrow, OK*

Helper's Seat Cushion

Designate a child to be your special helper during circle time. Then give your helper a unique seat cushion to spotlight his special job. Simply obtain a mouse pad with a fun print. Then encourage the youngster to sit on the mouse pad. *Sarah Booth, Messiah Nursery School, South Williamsport, PA*

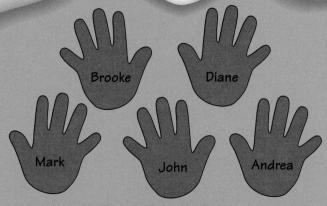

Easy Handprints

At the beginning of the school year, trace each youngster's hand onto tagboard and then personalize and cut out each tracing. Store the cutouts in a file. Then, whenever you need a handprint cutout, just trace the template! *Michele Van Buren, Morrison Community Day Care, Morrison, IL*

Movable Nametags

Use these nametags at snacktime, at lunchtime, or for any activity where youngsters need to take their seats at a table! Simply make a stand-up nametag similar to the one shown for each child; then place a nametag on the table in front of each seat. *Pam Booher and Connie Farmer, Early Childhood Center, Franklin, KY*

Daily Organization

Obtain five medium plastic containers and label each one with a different day of the school week. Then organize the props and materials you need for each day in the containers. You'll save time by having everything you need right at hand! *Carol Allen, Harvest Christian Preschool, Griffin, GA*

Management Tips & Timesavers

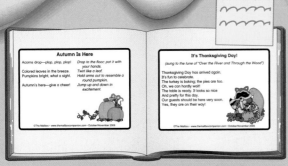

Splendid Song Cards

For each song and rhyme in the "Songs and Such" department of *The Mailbox*® magazine, there is a card available for printing at themailboxcompanion.com! Store these cards in a 4" x 6" photo album. Simply use sticky notes as dividers to label sections based on theme or skill. You'll have oodles of activities at your fingertips. *Delores Spagnuolo, Grandmama's Preschool, Topeka, KS*

Simple Labeling

Attach address labels you receive in the mail to all the items in the classroom that are your personal property. With these handy labels, items that are loaned to other teachers are sure to be returned. Also, if you change classrooms or schools, it's easy to tell which items belong to you. *Lisa Myers, Newport Grammar School, Newport, TN*

Sprinkle Control

If your glitter shakers are pouring glitter rather than sprinkling it, simply place a piece of tape on the shaker so that it covers some of the holes. There will be less glitter wasted, and projects will still sparkle and shine. *Linda Bille, Riviera United Methodist Preschool, Redondo Beach, CA*

Cleanup Freeze

To motivate youngsters during cleanup time, play a recording of upbeat music. Then, while students are cleaning, periodically pause the music and encourage youngsters to freeze. You'll hear lots of giggles during this fun and productive cleanup time. *Christine Badey, Hamilton Avenue Early Childhood Center, Trenton, NJ*

Just Like Magic!

Here's an easy way to remove permanent marker from laminated posters or nametags. Dampen a Mr. Clean Magic Eraser cleaning pad; then gently rub it over the ink. Presto—the marker is removed! *Janet Woodard, Stepping Stones Preschool, Sylvania, OH*

Management Tips & Timesavers

Photo File

You'll have student photos at your fingertips with this simple idea! Label index card dividers with student names. Then place the cards in a shoebox. Whenever you have extra photographs of youngsters, file them in the box. This way, whenever you need a photo for a project or an activity, you can find what you need immediately. *Eileen Gingras, The Children's School at Deerfield Academy, Deerfield, MA*

Easy Cleanup

Before youngsters begin potentially messy art projects, place a vinyl tablecloth on your art table. When each child has completed the project, simply toss the tablecloth in the washing machine. What an easy cleanup! *Barbara Lamb, Orange County Head Start, Orange, VA*

Multipurpose Containers

Plastic baby food containers with snap-on lids are super handy in the classroom! Gather a container for each child and then use them as personal glue holders. They are also handy for holding small amounts of paint, as well as for storing items such as stickers. *Missy Goldenberg, Beth Shalom Preschool, Overland Park, KS*

Clothing Carrier

Place extra changes of clothing for your youngsters in a see-through over-the-door shoe carrier. Each section can easily be labeled with a youngster's name. And since the carrier is transparent, you can see at a glance if any items of clothing need replacing. *Marie Altavilla, St. Anne School, Columbus, GA*

Word of the Day

During your morning routine, help students decide on a special word for the day. Then, throughout the day, have students wait for the special word before completing certain tasks, such as coming to circle time or lining up. *Saundra Sweeney, Tuskawilla Presbyterian Preschool, Oviedo, FL*

Management Tips & Timesavers

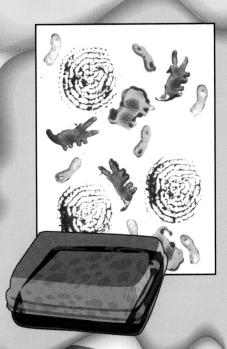

Homemade Stamp Pads

To make this handy stamp pad, place a damp sponge in a plastic container with a lid. Then squeeze washable paint over the sponge. After a child uses the stamp pad, attach the lid and store it until the next stamping project. *Mary Bukowski, Our Lady of the Wayside School, Arlington Heights, IL; Martha Whitaker, Loving Start Preschool, Milwaukee, WI*

No Building Zone

This simple idea keeps students' block creations safe from youngsters trying to remove other blocks from the block shelf. Use a length of masking tape to make a parallel line two feet from your block shelf. Designate the area between the tape and the shelf as a "No Building Zone." *Cathy Consford, Buda Primary Early Learning Center, Buda, TX*

Compliment Jar

Decorate a clear plastic jar and place a supply of pom-poms near it. Anytime a compliment is given by you, an adult helper, or a student, place a pom-pom in the jar. When the jar is full, reward students with a special treat or privilege. *Linda Solomon, George Washington Carver Elementary, Solon, OH*

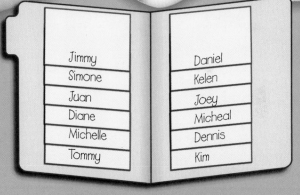

Flip Chart Recording

Keeping anecdotal records of your students is a snap with this quick-to-make chart. Tape a class supply of index cards inside a file folder as shown. Then label each card with a different child's name. Simply flip to the appropriate card and jot notes pertaining to that student. *Brenda Taylor, Mae Stevens Elementary, Copperas Cove, TX*

Line Up

Help little ones line up correctly when coming in from outdoor play. Place a decorative stepping-stone where you want the line to begin. The line leader stands on the stepping-stone and his classmates line up behind him. *Dot Stein, Christian Beginnings Preschool, Prince Frederick, MD*

Management Tips & Timesavers

Games Made Simple

Make homemade matching games in a flash with this tip! Program pairs of juice can lids (game pieces) with matching pictures, letters, or numbers. Then store the game pieces in a cylindrical potato chip container. They fit perfectly! *Sarah Palmberg, Friendship Day Care, Hutchinson, KS*

M   m

Smooth Moves

Transition to centers with ease and review rhyming words at the same time! Lead youngsters in chanting, "Center time, center time, time to make a rhyme!" Announce a word and then have a child name a rhyming word and transition to his desired center. Continue in this manner until each student is at a center. *Jodi McNamara, Kids 'R' Kids #49, Lawrenceville, GA*

Great Job!

Instead of having students add stickers to a personalized reward chart, have them mark good behavior with a shape puncher. After a student punches her chart a predetermined number of times, she receives a special prize or privilege! *Carrie Riebel, Marmaton Valley School, Moran, KS*

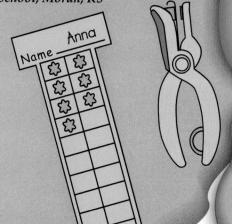

Get on Board

Lining up on the playground is a snap with this idea. Make a class supply of train car cutouts. When it is time to line up on the playground, signal your little ones by blowing a train whistle. As each child lines up, give him a train car. Then have the line of students chug along until they arrive at the classroom. *Anne Plagge, Hampton Community Christian Day Care, Hampton, IA*

No More Missing Pieces

To easily find the homes of stray puzzle pieces, label each puzzle box or tray with a letter and then write the same letter on the back of each corresponding puzzle piece. When a piece is found, simply return it to the appropriate puzzle. *Nancy Simson, Barlow School, Plainfield, NJ*

SCIENCE EXPLORATIONS

Science

Where Is Air?
Youngsters can't see air, but they can prove that it's there with this simple experiment.

STEP 1

Gather a small group of youngsters and have them stand and twirl around with their arms outstretched. Ask them to describe what they feel, leading them to conclude that they can feel air rushing past their arms as they twirl.

STEP 2

There is air in the block center.

Explain to students that air is everywhere. To reinforce this, have each student name places where there is air, such as under the table, in the hallway, in the classroom, and on the playground.

STEP 5

?

Tape the dog in the cup once again and lower it into the water. Ask students what they think will happen if you tilt the cup.

STEP 6

Tilt the cup, prompting students to watch as the air bubbles leave the cup and the water rushes in. Remove the cup from the water and pass around the dog once again. Guide youngsters to realize that when the air left the cup, the water was able to come in, so the dog got wet.

Explorations

To explore air, you will need the following:
clear plastic cup
large clear container of water
dog cutout
tape

STEP 3

He'll get wet!

Tell students that they cannot see air but they can do something to capture it. Have students watch as you tip the cup upside down and tape the dog cutout inside the cup. Give the dog a name, such as Spot, and then tell youngsters that Spot doesn't like to take a bath. Ask youngsters what will happen to the dog if you lower the cup into the container of water.

STEP 4

Lower the glass into the water as youngsters watch. Then bring the glass straight out of the water. Remove the cutout from the glass and have youngsters feel it to determine whether it is wet or dry. When they discover that it is dry, explain that the air in the glass kept the water from getting in, so Spot stayed dry.

Did You Know?

The air in an average-size room weighs around 75 pounds. We don't feel the air's weight because the air is spread out around us.

What Now?

Experiment with a different way to trap air. Give each child a resealable bag. Help the child capture air in the bag and then seal it. Then invite students to gently squeeze the bags and toss them to their classmates. They've captured bagfuls of air!

Plastic Bags

Science

Beautiful Bones

Youngsters get the scoop on skeletons with this simple exploration!

STEP 1

Gather a small group of students. Then have each youngster feel one of his arms. Encourage him to discuss what he feels, prompting him to conclude that the hard material he feels in his arm is a bone.

STEP 2

The bones in my hand are small!

Encourage each child to feel other parts of his body—such as his spine, legs, and hands—for bones. Then prompt students to discuss what they feel. Encourage students to feel for bones that are long, such as their leg bones; bones that are curved, such as their ribs; and bones that are small, such as their finger bones.

STEP 5

A lion has bones.

Have students suggest other creatures that have bones, such as cats, dogs, and mice. If desired, take the opportunity to explain that some animals, like the octopus, have no bones at all!

STEP 6

Finally, tell students that it's important to keep their bones healthy. They can do this by exercising. Lead students through several jumping jacks and other exercises. Further explain that eating certain foods, such as dairy products, can keep their bones healthy as well. End your exploration of bones with a snack of milk and cheese.

Explorations

To explore bones, you will need the following:
magnifying glass
chicken bone, cooked and cleaned
dairy snack, such as milk and cheese, for each child

STEP 3

Tell students that the bones inside them help support them and give them shape. Without their bones, they would be floppy and saggy! Prompt youngsters to flop about as if they have no bones.

STEP 4

It's brown and bumpy on the ends.

Ask youngsters to describe what they think their bones look like. After they share their suggestions, show youngsters the chicken bone. Have students use the magnifying glass to observe the bone. Then prompt them to describe what they see.

Did You Know?

Babies have about 300 bones in their bodies. As people grow older, some of the bones fuse together. By the time they reach adulthood, they will only have about 206 bones!

What Now?

Explain to students that their skeletons are mostly made of bone, but some parts are made of cartilage. Cartilage isn't as hard as bone, and it can move and bend. Have students gently press their noses and ears to feel the cartilage.

Science

Salt and Sugar

With this sweet investigation, youngsters use their senses to explore salt and sugar!

STEP 1

Gather a small group of students and show them bowl 1 and bowl 2. Have students predict whether the substances in the bowls are the same or different.

STEP 2

Draw two columns on the chart paper and label the columns "1" and "2," respectively. Have youngsters look at the salt and sugar. As they describe each substance, write down their descriptive words in the appropriate column.

STEP 5

Invite each youngster to taste a few grains of sugar. Then repeat the process with the salt. Encourage students to describe how the substances taste. Write youngsters' descriptive words on the chart. Then help youngsters guess the name of the substance in each bowl.

STEP 6

Tell students that salt and sugar are used in many different foods. Give each child a salty snack and a sweet snack, such as a potato chip and a cookie. Encourage each child to nibble on his snack and explain which snack is sweet and which is salty.

Explorations

To explore salt and sugar, you will need the following:
small bowl of salt, labeled "1"
small bowl of sugar, labeled "2"
chart paper
marker
salty snack (one per child)
sweet snack (one per child)
napkin (one per child)

STEP 3

This one feels bumpier!

Have each child feel both the salt and the sugar. Invite students to describe how the substances feel. Then write any additional descriptive words on the chart.

STEP 4

Invite students to smell both the salt and the sugar. Once again, write any descriptive words on the chart.

Did You Know?

When salt is sprinkled on ice, the ice will melt at a lower temperature than normal. This is why salt is often spread on icy walkways and roads.

What Now?

Have more fun with salt and sugar! Have students place an egg in each of two glasses of water and watch it sink. Remove the eggs and have students mix ten tablespoons of salt in one glass and ten tablespoons of sugar in another glass. When the salt and sugar have dissolved, place the eggs back in the glasses. Amazingly, the eggs will float!

Science Explorations

Instant Attraction

Youngsters investigate the strength of magnets with this attractive exploration!

idea contributed by Missy Goldenberg
Beth Shalom Nursery School, Overland Park, KS

Materials:
strong magnet for each child
jumbo paper clips
bottle of water
container of sand
copy of the recording sheet on page 112
   for each youngster

STEP 1

Give each child a magnet and a recording sheet. Display a pile of paper clips. Ask youngsters if they think the magnet will attract the paper clips. After each child shares his thoughts, have him wave his magnet over the paper clips. Then prompt him to circle the appropriate picture on his paper to show that the magnet attracts the paper clips.

STEP 2

Next, nestle paper clips in a shallow container of sand. Then drop paper clips in the bottle of water and secure the cap.

STEP 3

Ask students if they think the magnet will attract the paper clips in the sand. After each youngster shares his thoughts, have him run his magnet over the top of the sand. Then have each child circle the appropriate picture to show that the magnet attracts the paper clips through the sand.

STEP 4

Finally, hold up the bottle of water and ask students if they think the magnet will attract the paper clips through the plastic and water. After each child shares his prediction, have him run his magnet over the bottle, noticing that the paper clips move toward the magnet. Have each youngster circle the appropriate picture on his paper to record the results.

What Now?

Line the bottom of your water table (or a plastic tub) with paper. Place paint-covered magnetic marbles in the tub. Then have students move magnets along the bottom of the tub, moving the marbles to make a lovely painting. When students are finished, clean and store the marbles for safekeeping.

110

Which Food Is Healthier?

Lift the flaps to see!

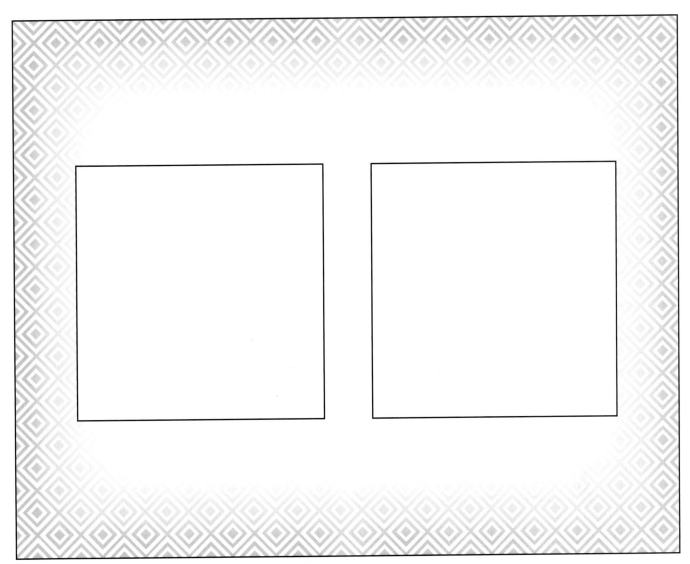

Note to the teacher: Use with "Greasy Grub" on page 109. Have each child cut out the cards and then tape each one to a different box on the paper towel to make two flaps. Prompt her to draw a spot underneath the appropriate flap to reflect the result of the experiment.

What Happened?

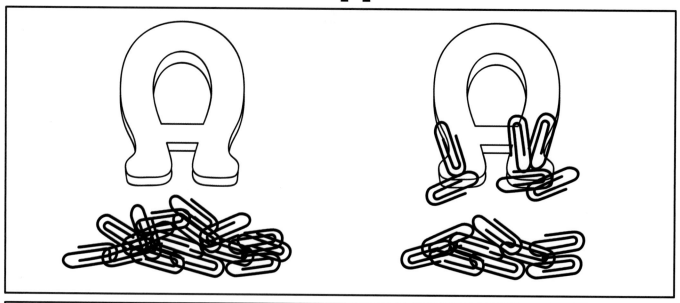

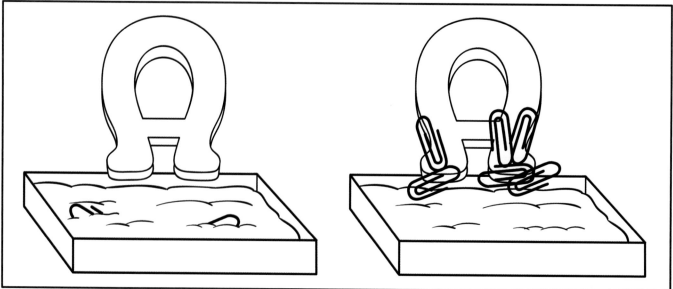

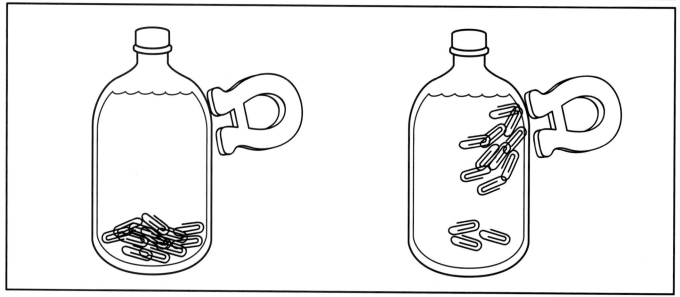

Note to the teacher: Use with "Instant Attraction" on page 110.

OUR READERS WRITE

Our Readers Write

Hi!
I am tickled pink to have you in my class! We are going to have a wonderful year. We will start the year by learning about nursery rhymes and fairy tales. It will be so much fun!

I hope to see you at our open house on Tuesday, August 14, at 6:30 P.M.

Love,
Ms. Dills and friends

Tweety Bird

Hoppy Toad

Perfectly Pink

I send a fun letter like the one shown to each student before our open house. I write a simple letter welcoming my students to preschool and telling them about our classroom themes. I sign the letter with my name as well as the names of my classroom pets. Then I copy the letter onto attractive stationery for each child. Before sending out the letters, I tuck a pink feather into each envelope!

Janet Dills, Rejoice Christian School, Owasso, OK

Simple Centering

I use a pencil to make a small mark in the center of all of my bulletin board frames. With this simple guideline it's easy to center display materials and bulletin board titles on all the boards I create throughout the year.

Isobel L. Livingstone, Rahway, NJ

I love you. Have a good day!

You are a terrific preschooler!

Framed Photos

I give my housekeeping area a homey look with framed photos! Enlarge a class photo and other student photos. Laminate the photos and then attach a frame to each photo. (Make sure the frames do not contain glass.) Mount the framed photos to walls in your housekeeping area. They look picture-perfect!

Dayle Timmons
Jacksonville, FL

WELCOME

Mommy Notes

To help youngsters who are sad about saying goodbye to their families, I've created a jar of mommy notes. (These can also be called daddy notes or grandma notes, depending on the title of the youngster's primary caregiver.) I write special messages, such as those shown, on each of several colorful notes and then place them in a decorated container. If a youngster is feeling particularly upset when he says goodbye to his caregiver, I have him choose a note. I explain that the note is a happy thought from his caregiver and me and then I read aloud the message. These notes have always provided a great deal of comfort to my youngsters.

Carol Allen, Harvest Christian Preschool
Griffin, GA

Simple Seasonal Crowns

These unique birthday crowns are always popular with my little ones. I make four die-cuts of shapes that relate to the current season. I label them with the word *Happy,* the word *Birthday,* the youngster's name, and her age. Then I attach the cutouts to a length of construction paper with zigzag detailing. Simply size the resulting crown to fit the child's head.

Cindy Kelley
St. Bernard Catholic School
Wabash, IN

Daily Calendar Pages

I always keep a cute daily desk calendar in my classroom. Near the end of the school day, I rip off the current day's page. Then I write a brief note on the page highlighting something positive about one of my students. I send home this very special page with the corresponding youngster. My little ones always enjoy getting the calendar page to take home!

Vicki Ault, Guiding Hand Preschool, Cheshire, OH

Supersize Photos

These supersize student photos look terrific on lockers or as a permanent display in the classroom. I take a full-body digital photo of each child. I enlarge the upper half of the photo to fit on an 8" x 10" sheet of paper and then print out the photo. I repeat the process with the lower half. After I cut out the two halves, I tape them together and laminate them for durability. These photos always get lots of compliments!

Karen Brandt, McCarroll Early Childhood Center
Ottumwa, IA

Lovely Holders

To make these attractive holders, I center a coffee can on a 14-inch square of cloth. I pull the cloth around the can and secure it with a rubber band. After I adjust the fabric to conceal the rubber band, I fill the can with paintbrushes, pencils, or even plastic flowers. These cans really brighten up our room.

Isobel L. Livingstone
Rahway, NJ

Monthly Memories

I like to make this keepsake book with my students! At the end of each month throughout the school year, I take a photograph of each child. Then I give her the photo and a sheet of construction paper with the month's name written across the top. She glues her photo to the paper and then decorates the paper with stickers or cutouts relating to the themes we studied that month. At the end of the school year, I bind each child's pages together to make a book she can take home!

Rebecca Hirsch, Redeemer Lutheran Nursery School, Queens Village, NY

Our Readers Write

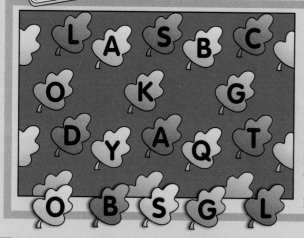

Gift Wrap Games

I use gift wrap to make simple matching games! When I find gift wrap with a large pattern, I mount the gift wrap on poster board and then program it with letters or numbers. I use additional gift wrap to make matching game pieces. Then I laminate the poster board and game pieces for durability. Students place the game pieces over the matching symbols on the poster board. I'm always looking for gift wrap that matches the seasons and my themes!

Marti Smith, McKinley Elementary, Lisbon, OH

Classroom Quilt

I always get compliments on this environmental print wall display! I cut the front panels from food boxes and then trim the panels to equal sizes. I punch holes along the edges of each panel. I help the students use yarn to lace the panels together and then display the finished quilt. My youngsters love to identify the different food items!

Ann Larberg, DeLand, FL

Texas Turkeys

Our youngsters love making this supersize turkey. Obtain a class supply of Liquid Watercolor Big Texas Snowflakes coffee filters. This extra large filter has a diameter of 23½ inches! We help each child use an eyedropper to drip tinted water on a filter. When the filter dries, youngsters attach turkey bodies, feet, and facial features to their projects. Then we display these jumbo turkeys in the hallway!

Teresa Mastin and Jannell Wallace
Ascension Christian Preschool
Citrus Heights, CA

Apple Surprise!

My little ones enjoy celebrating fall with this twist on a favorite treat! I slide craft sticks into a class supply of apples and use our microwave to prepare a bowl of melted caramel. I carefully supervise each child as she dips her apple into the caramel and then places it on a sheet of waxed paper. Then I encourage each child to press a few gummy worms into the caramel. My youngsters really love snacking on this sweet treat!

Keely Peasner, Liberty Ridge Head Start
Bonney Lake, WA

Milk Jug Jack-o'-Lanterns

Our fall festival is extra special with these decorations! I have each youngster paint a clean milk jug with a mixture of orange paint and glue. When the jug is dry, I have the student glue precut shapes to the jug to make a face. Right before our classroom party, I place a glow stick in the bottom of each jug. It's so festive!

Lindsey Strickland, L. P. Waters ECLC
Greenville, TX

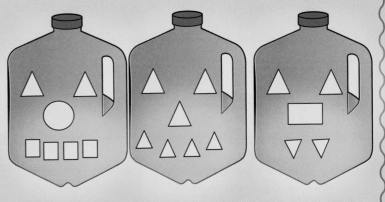

Pumpkin Puzzles

Here's a fun way for youngsters to learn about each other's families. I cut a large pumpkin shape from orange poster board and then cut the pumpkin into a class supply of puzzle pieces. I have each child take a puzzle piece home and decorate it with family photos and fall-related items. When all the pieces have been returned to school, I help youngsters assemble the pumpkin and attach it to bulletin board paper. Then I cut it out and mount it on a wall.

Karen Dikeman, First Presbyterian Little School
Kokomo, IN

Falling Leaves

This idea really gives my classroom that fall feeling! I take my little ones on a nature walk and have them collect different types of leaves to bring back to the classroom. I attach poster board branches to the ceiling and then suspend the leaves on fishing wire so they appear to be falling to the ground.

Christina Hossack, Little Wonders Day School
Jamesburg, NJ

Thumbprint Trees

To make these cute trees, I have each child attach a tree cutout to the left side of a sheet of construction paper. Then he makes thumbprint leaves using different fall-colored paints. When the paint is dry, I attach on the remaining side of the paper a copy of the poem shown. This project makes a wonderful keepsake!

Sondra Lougee

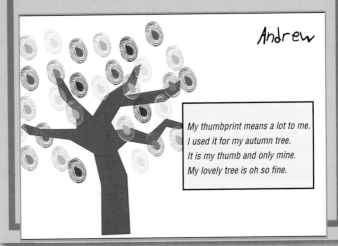

Andrew

My thumbprint means a lot to me.
I used it for my autumn tree.
It is my thumb and only mine.
My lovely tree is oh so fine.

Spin Art

Try this idea for an inexpensive way to make spin art! To eliminate the cost of buying a traditional spin art wheel, I bought a lazy Susan. I cut a piece of paper to size and then attached it to the wheel with a small piece of Sticky-Tac. It's simple to spin the wheel as youngsters paint.

Jennifer Avegno, Carousel Preschool, Cypress, CA

Our Readers Write

Simple Wrapping

Instead of using gift wrap when wrapping gifts to parents, I have my youngsters use aluminum foil! It's simple for their little hands to fold the foil over the gift and they don't have to use any tape. The foil stays put and looks quite lovely with a gift tag and a festive bow.

Peggy Nelson, Will Rogers United Methodist Preschool, Tulsa, OK

Snack Tip

My youngsters' families provide snacks for my preschool class. To give parents fun, healthy snack options, I make a copy of the "Kids in the Kitchen" department in each issue of *The Mailbox®* magazine I own. Then I bind the copies together and attach the finished book to my parent message board outside my classroom. Parents love to flip through the book for simple, kid-friendly recipes.

Jennifer Schear, Clover Patch Preschool, Cedar Falls, IA

Dear Family,

Please enjoy the items in this bag over the weekend. The items will need to be returned on January 10, 2008. We would love for you to add comments about your experiences with the items to the "Family Comments" notebook!

This bag contains the following:
Snowmen at Night by Caralyn Buehner
Time to Sleep by Denise Fleming
The Snowy Day by Ezra Jack Keats
A mitten-matching game mat and 20 mitten cards

Kindness Chains

At the beginning of December, I recognize a child who has done a simple act of kindness in the classroom. I have that child make a loop from a strip of construction paper; then I attach the loop to a bulletin board. Each time I notice a student being kind, I have him add a loop to the previous loop to make a chain. My youngsters love to watch this chain grow!

Suzanne Maxymuk, Evergreen Avenue School, Woodbury, NJ

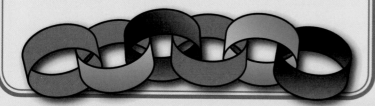

Family Fun Bag

To make a family fun bag, I use fabric paint to decorate a tote bag. Then I place several picture books and games in the bag. (Often these items relate to a theme we are studying.) I also put in the bag a notebook titled "Family Comments." I place a note in the bag explaining the items included and when the bag should be returned. Then I send the bag home with a youngster. I've heard nothing but good comments from parents about this fun home-school connection.

Elizabeth Laitman, River Grove School
River Grove, IL

Baked With Love

Mix and measure,
Stir and bake.
Not a pie, not a cake.
Baked with love
Through and through.
Here's a gift from me to you!
Andy

For a special family holiday gift, I help my youngsters whip up batches of cookies. We place a few cookies on a colorful disposable plate for each student's family. We cover the plate with plastic wrap and then top the present with a bow and the adorable poem shown.

Cindy Anderson
Shining Star Pre-School
Middletown, RI

Pocket Change

Here's a simple way for youngsters to help others during the holiday season. I had youngsters and their families work together to donate any desired pocket change for a period of three weeks. We then arranged a very special field trip! We went to the bank, where youngsters watched the change being counted and exchanged for paper money. Then we went to the toy store, where my youngsters selected several toys to purchase for less fortunate children.

Aimee Robertson, School for Little People, Sherman, TX

Flannel Shapes

I recently discovered that die-cut machines can cut felt shapes as well as paper shapes! I can now quickly make flannelboard activities to go with songs and rhymes. I can also punch out shapes to make simple flannelboard games.

Jacinda Roberts, Little Early Childhood Center, Wichita, KS

Student Snowflakes

It's easy to make these personalized snowflakes! I use my digital camera to take a photograph of each child. Then I print each photo in the center of a sheet of paper. I fold the paper to make a snowflake. After I cut desired pieces and notches out of the paper, I open the paper and display the resulting snowflake in the classroom.

Tammy Parks
Treehouse Daycare
Grandville, MI

A Measurement Tree

For a fun holiday measurement activity, I attach a supersize holiday tree cutout to a wall. (Make sure the tree is quite wide.) I have each child stand against the tree; then I make a mark on the tree to show the height of the child. I measure the height of the mark and then I write the height and child's name on a simple student-made paper ornament. I attach the ornament to the tree over the original mark. I add ornaments for adult helpers and other teachers to ensure an evenly decorated tree.

Meg Thaler, Scarsdale Congregational Church Nursery School, Scarsdale, NY

The Education Center®

The **MAILBOX.**
Be the difference:

Our Readers Write

Bright Idea

Here's a simple way to make a light table for your classroom. I drill several holes in the sides of an oversize clear plastic storage container, making sure that one hole is large enough for the plug to pass through. (The smaller holes are for ventilation.) I put strings of white holiday lights inside the container and pull the plug through the largest hole. After placing the lid on the container, I flip the container over and plug in the lights. I place the resulting light table in a center along with colorful translucent props. My students love to place the props on the table and watch them light up.

Louise McKnight
Children's Cottage Early Learning Center
Anacortes, WA

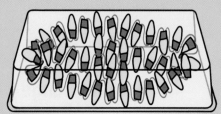

Marching for March

My youngsters quickly learn the name of the month of March with this fun idea! During calendar time, I prompt students to announce the name of the month. Once we establish that the month is March, I invite a youngster to hold a baton and lead the class in a march around the room while I play a recording of marching band music.

Elizabeth Cook
King of Kings Lutheran
Mason, OH

Pleasing Postcards

Colorful postcards are popular in my centers! Whenever I travel, I buy a variety of postcards. Then I place a few laminated postcards at a center. Students build vocabulary by discussing the pictures on the postcards or sorting the postcards as desired. This is always a popular center option.

Susan Bumgarner
Wilson Arts Integration Elementary
Oklahoma City, OK

Refrigerator Art

When I run out of space in the classroom to display students' artwork, I use painter's tape to create the outline of a huge refrigerator on the wall in our corridor. Then I tape the artwork inside the outline. This unique display results in smiles from both students and classroom visitors.

Rosemary Keese
Little People Playtime
Hampshire, IL

Fun at the Fence

I discovered that plastic cups fit perfectly in the holes of a chain-link fence. During outdoor play, I give a student a tub with cups and letter cards. He chooses a card and inserts the cups in the fence to form the letter. I've used this activity with numbers, shapes, and patterns as well!

Tammy Kuehl
Trinity-St. Luke's Lutheran School
Watertown, WI

Lights for All

To help ease students' fears during a thunderstorm, I keep a supply of small, inexpensive flashlights. When a storm is coming, I give each student a flashlight to hold or keep in her pocket. This way, if the power goes out, the students are prepared. Now my little ones look forward to thunderstorms!

Paula Beckerman, Paula's Preschool
Arlington, TX

Tuned In to Books

With this easy tip, I transform a classic book into a musical masterpiece! Read aloud *Brown Bear, Brown Bear, What Do You See?* by Bill Martin Jr. Then revisit the book and lead youngsters in singing the words to the tune of "Twinkle, Twinkle, Little Star." The words fit perfectly with this traditional tune!

Tammy Stapley, The Preschool Club, Eugene, OR

Swirled Colors

I found a simple way to brighten a rainy day! I have each student put on his rain gear and then I give him a plastic plate with several drops of food coloring in two primary colors. Once outside, a student catches some raindrops on his plate and then watches the food coloring swirl together to make a new color.

Nicole Furfaro, St. Paul Catholic School
Guelph, Ontario, Canada

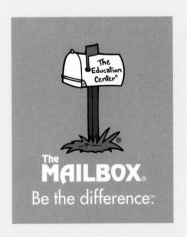

The MAILBOX.
Be the difference.™

Rain Bottles

My youngsters love manipulating these glittery props when we sing our favorite songs about rain. To make one, I have each child put sequins and silver, blue, and white glitter in a clear pint-size water bottle. Then, using a funnel, I help him add blue-tinted water to his bottle. I secure the cap and then reinforce it with tape.

Sarah Weingartz, Small Wonders Preschool/District 194
Lakeville, MN

Our Readers Write

What's in the Can?

To introduce a thematic unit, I place a small theme-related object in a decorated coffee can. During circle time, we pass the can, allowing each child to shake it while we sing "What's in the Can?" to the tune of "Here Comes the Bride." Students guess what is in the can before I ask one child to remove the lid and reveal the object.

Tina Torello
Honey Tree Learning Center
Hanson, MA

Jigsaw Success

My students who have motor difficulties often get frustrated trying to finish a puzzle. To help them feel successful, I put together a portion of the puzzle and then glue it in place. A youngster places the remaining pieces and he's finished a puzzle all by himself.

Erin Rawls
Skipwith Elementary
Richmond, VA

Garden Angels

I always get a lot of compliments for this Mother's Day gift. I cut out a photograph of each youngster wearing a garland halo and then glue it to a jumbo craft stick with the sign shown. I have each student sponge-paint a clay pot. Then I help him plant a brightly colored flower in the pot and insert the stick behind the flower.

Garden Angel

Kathi Delp
Grace Episcopal Day School
Orange Park, FL

Stained Glass Pictures

I found a quick and easy way to help youngsters make this familiar art project. I lightly spray a piece of waxed paper with cooking spray. Then I have a student place pieces of tissue paper on the waxed paper. The tissue paper sticks to the spray! Next, I smooth a second piece of waxed paper over the first and staple the project in a construction paper frame.

Laurie Hasson
B'nai Israel Schilit Nursery School
Rockville, MD

Our Readers Write

Fuzzy Puppet Friends

These humorous puppets are simple to make! I purchase shaggy car-washing mitts in several colors. Then I attach a pair of jumbo wiggle eyes to each mitt. These puppets are favorites among the students in my class!

Tammy Floyd
Calvary Baptist Kindergarten
Florence, SC

Candy Mold Creations

To make easy seasonal magnets, I have each of my little ones press Crayola Model Magic modeling compound into an inexpensive candy mold. I remove the cast from each mold and set it aside. When the compound is dry, the students decorate the casts using markers or tempera paints. Then I attach a magnet to the back of each cast.

Kasi Horwart
Fingerprints Preschool
Cambridge, NE

Nifty Noodles

This fun flower arrangement really brightens up my classroom! I cut a swimming pool noodle into several pieces. I arrange the pieces and then wrap clear tape around them to hold them in place. My youngsters love to slide plastic flowers into the resulting vases!

Amy R. Monahan
St. Anthony's Health Center
Alton, IL

Happy Father's Day!

Dad's Wallet

This cute project makes a wonderful Father's Day gift. For each child, I fold a 9" x 12" sheet of paper as shown and add a border that resembles stitching. Then I have the child attach small drawings or photographs to the resulting wallet. When a youngster's father opens his wallet, he will find treasures that are greater than money.

Karen Eiben
The Learning House Preschool
La Salle, IL

Cake Decorations

A couple of weeks before our preschool graduation ceremony, we take a photograph of each student wearing his cap and gown. We cut out each photo and attach it to a wooden craft stick. Then we insert the sticks into the cake we serve after the graduation ceremony. Students and parents absolutely love this decorated dessert!

Jane Vogt and Jackie Miller
Cleveland Child Care
Cleveland, OH

Sleds in the Summer

For years I only used sleds in the winter, but now I have a great way to use them in the summer as well! I place plastic sleds in our outdoor play area. I fill some of the sleds with water. My little ones can sit in the dry sleds and pretend they're boating, or they can play with plastic toys in the water-filled sleds.

Karen Eiben
The Learning House Preschool
La Salle, IL

Chair Wash

To make my classroom chairs look new again, I take them to the local self-service car wash. I line the chairs up and use the pressure spray with a little soap to remove a year's worth of crayon, glue, and paint. Then I towel-dry them or let them dry in the sun.

Jodi Reiner
St. Catherine's of Siena Preschool
Carrollton, TX

My Teacher and Me

To make this school-year memento, I make a handprint on a sheet of construction paper labeled "My Teacher and Me." Then I have a child make a handprint in a contrasting color near my handprint. Finally, I attach a photo of myself with the child. This project makes a wonderful keepsake.

Karen Meyers, First Baptist Preschool, Long Beach, MS

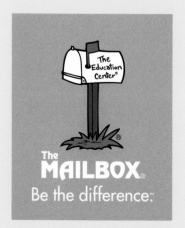

Summer Fun Kit

At the end of the school year, I create a summer fun kit for each student. I place in a gift bag a recording of familiar music, handmade props, matching games, and a description of how to use the materials. This kit gives parents several fun activities to do with their little ones over the summer break.

Sheila Halsey Scott
Grassfield Elementary
Chesapeake, VA

STORYTIME

Storytime

School Bus
Written and illustrated by Donald Crews

With simple text and vivid illustrations, this eye-catching book follows school buses throughout their busy day.

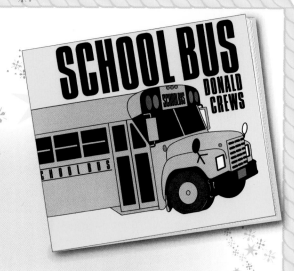

Good morning, Wyatt!

Bus Stop

Before You Read
Invite youngsters to ride an imaginary school bus! Assign groups of children to different mock bus stop areas in your classroom. Then pretend to drive the imaginary bus to each area, welcoming children aboard as you go. At the end of the bus ride, unload your youngsters at your group-time area to settle in for a read-aloud about a day in the life of a school bus.

After You Read
Here's a fun, interactive rereading of the story! Make a large school bus cutout from yellow bulletin board paper. Attach the bus to a wall at students' eye level. Give each child a person cutout and have her decorate it so it resembles herself. Place Sticky-Tac on the back of each cutout. Reread the story aloud. When the buses pick up the children, have each student attach her cutout to the bus. When the buses unload the youngsters, prompt each child to remove her cutout.

Cookie's Week

Written by Cindy Ward
Illustrated by Tomie dePaola

Cookie the cat gets into a different kind of mischief almost every day of the week. No doubt the lively action in this story will enchant your little ones!

ideas contributed by Janet Boyce
Cokato, MN

Before You Read

Youngsters name the days of the week with this little ditty. After singing several rounds, invite your little ones to listen to this action-packed read-aloud about a cat who gets into trouble almost every day of the week.

(sung to the tune of "Clementine")

Sunday, Monday,
Tuesday, Wednesday,
Thursday, Friday, Saturday.
We've just named the days of the week.
Everybody shout, "Hooray!"
Hooray!

After You Read

Write a different day on each of seven cards and then display the cards in a row, beginning with Monday. Color and cut out a copy of the picture cards on page 136. Ask youngsters what mischief Cookie gets into on Monday. (Use the book's illustrations as a guide if needed.) Then have a student choose the appropriate card and attach it below the Monday card. Continue in the same way with each remaining day.

Storytime

Bear Snores On

Written by Karma Wilson
Illustrated by Jane Chapman

While Bear takes his winter nap, forest animals take shelter in his nice warm cave. Their impromptu party eventually wakes Bear, but instead of being angry with his uninvited guests, he just wants to be included in the fun!

ideas contributed by Tricia Kylene Brown,
Brown's Academy for Boys Homeschool, Bowling Green, KY

Before You Read

This prereading activity is sure to cause oodles of giggles! Show youngsters the cover of the book and then read aloud the title. Ask students what a bear might sound like when it snores. Then have little ones demonstrate their best bear snores. After several moments, give youngsters a round of applause for their playacting. Then explain that the bear in the book snores through a party right in his own cave! Finally, have students settle in for this fun read-aloud!

After You Read

Who came to seek shelter in the cave? Youngsters will be eager to tell you with this story review. Attach a construction paper cave to a wall in your classroom. Color and cut out a copy of the animal cards on page 137 and place the cards in a bag. Have a youngster choose a card and name the animal. Encourage youngsters to explain whether the animal is one found in the story, using the illustrations in the book as needed. If the animal is found in the story, have a youngster attach the card to the cave. If it is not, have her set the card aside. Continue in the same way with the remaining cards.

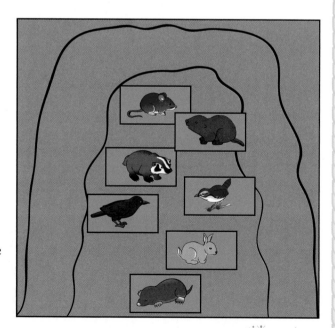

Snow

Written and illustrated by Uri Shulevitz

*Snow-free forecasts don't hamper a boy's
enthusiasm as he and his dog watch tiny
snowflakes fall from the sky. One snowflake leads
to another, and soon the boy and his dog are
frolicking in the snow with magical friends.*

ideas contributed by Tricia Kylene Brown
Brown's Academy for Boys Homeschool, Bowling Green, KY

Before You Read

Make three snowflake cutouts (see page 283 for a snowflake pattern).
Then mount the snowflakes in plain view in your classroom. After youngsters are seated for storytime, dramatically exclaim that it's snowing. Have
youngsters look around the room until they can see all three snowflakes.
Then explain to students that some snowstorms, such as the one in the
story they're about to hear, begin with only a few snowflakes.

After You Read

The snowflakes in the story don't just fall to
the ground; they circle, swirl, twirl, dance, play,
and float. Prompt youngsters to pretend to be
snowflakes and move in the ways described.
Next, play a music recording and begin moving
like a snowflake. As you move, call on youngsters to join you until you have an entire class of
dancing, twirling snowflakes!

Storytime

Mouse's First Valentine
Written by Lauren Thompson
Illustrated by Buket Erdogan

Mouse watches his big sister scamper through the house. She's making something, but he doesn't know what it is. When his sister's project is finally done, she surprises Mouse with his very first valentine.

ideas contributed by Janet Boyce, Cokato, MN

Before You Read

Before little ones arrive, place lace, ribbon, glue, scissors, and a sheet of red paper in different areas of the classroom. After children are seated for storytime, walk around the room as if you are looking for something. Stop at each area to pick up the items and then bring them to the storytime area. Begin making a valentine and have youngsters guess what you are doing. Then explain that the mouse in the story you are about to read searches the house for the things she needs to make a valentine. Finally, have little ones settle in for this heartfelt read-aloud.

You're making a valentine!

Lee
I'm glad you're my friend!
Cassie

After You Read

Have little ones make a surprise valentine for a classmate! Place a name card for each child in a bag. Have each youngster pick a name from the bag. Encourage her to glue the name card to a large heart. Then have her dictate a message to the classmate for you to record on the heart. Encourage her to decorate this heartfelt valentine. Then gather little ones together for a special valentine exchange!

Sheep in a Jeep

Written by Nancy Shaw
Illustrated by Margot Apple

What begins as fun soon turns to trouble as these unlucky sheep take a jeep for a wool-raising ride! The rollicking rhymes and delightful illustrations are sure to induce lots of giggles from the little sheep in your flock!

Before You Read

Attach a large sheep cutout to a wall; then write the word *sheep* on the cutout (leave room to record rhyming words). To begin, tell little ones that the story you are about to read is filled with words that rhyme. Then help youngsters brainstorm words that rhyme with *sheep,* including nonsense words, and record the words on the drawing. As students settle in for this entertaining read-aloud, challenge them to see if any of the words in the story are the same as the words listed on the sheep.

After You Read

After youngsters listen to this delightful story about sheep in a jeep, have them make a new story about a pig in a rig! Make a copy of page 138 and attach it to a piece of chart paper. Introduce youngsters to the pig in a rig and then help students suggest words that rhyme with *pig.* Write their words below the picture. Then guide students in generating a story that uses the rhyming words. Write the story on the chart paper and then read it back to your little authors.

rig big wig jig twig dig fig

The pig had a rig.
The rig was big.
The pig wore a wig.
There was a twig in his wig.
He took out the twig.
Then he danced a jig.

138

©The Mailbox® • TEC41035 • Feb./Mar. 2008

Note to the teacher: Use with "After You Read" on page 131.

SONGS & SUCH

SONGS & SUCH

Five Little Leaves

This counting rhyme is sure to be "tree-mendously" fun for your little ones! Make five leaf cutouts; then give each leaf to a different child. Have the children stand in a row holding their leaves. Then lead students in reciting the chant, prompting the seated youngsters to move their arms back and forth to resemble the wind and encouraging one student to allow his leaf to fall to the floor. Repeat the process four more times, altering the numbers in the chant to reflect the remaining number of leaves.

[Five] little leaves, so happy and free,
Hung from a branch of a maple tree.
The wind came whistling all around,
And one little leaf came tumbling down.

Sandy Barker
Children's World
St. Paul, MN

The Friendly Scarecrow

Crows have nothing to fear from the scarecrow in this giggle-inducing song. Reduce the size of the crow pattern on page 92; then make a copy for each student. Have each child cut out his crow. Then lead students in singing the song and placing their crow cutouts on each body part mentioned.

(sung to the tune of "Mary Had a Little Lamb")

Scarecrow, scarecrow, there are crows
On your head, on your nose,
On your shoulders,
On your toes.
Please scare away those crows—boo!

adapted from a song by LeeAnn Collins
Sunshine House Preschool
Lansing, MI

Terrifi[c]

Lead students in performi[ng]
to be as quiet as mice! As st[udents]
their hands on their hips and

(sung to the tune of "I[...]")

Put your hands on your hips,
Put your hands on your hips,
Take your hands off your hip[s,]
Put your finger to your lips, t[o...]

Jillian Layne
Joyful Noises Preschool
Topsfield, MA

Apple on the Ground

Who's hiding in this little apple? Youngsters find out when they perform this cute rhyme! In advance, have each child paint a paper plate so it resembles an apple. Then cut in each apple craft a hole large enough to fit a child's finger. Give each child his apple; then guide students in performing the rhyme shown.

Apple, apple,
Juicy and round.

I found you lying on the ground.
I picked you up,
And what did I see?

A big fat worm looking right at me!

Hold up apple.
Run finger around outer
edge of apple.
Place apple on the floor.
Pick up apple.
Stick index finger
through the hole.
Wiggle finger.

LeeAnn Collins
Sunshine House Preschool
Lansing, MI

Outdoor Play

Lead little ones in singing this toe-tapping song as they march outdoors for playtime! If the day happens to be overcast, substitute the words *bright* and *sunny* in the fourth and sixth lines with the words *gray* and *cloudy*.

(sung to the tune of "The Ants Go Marching")

The kids go marching out to play. Hooray! Hooray!
The kids go marching out to play. Hooray! Hooray!
The kids go marching out to play
On this bright and sunny day.
And they all go marching
Out to play on this bright, sunny day.
Boom, boom, boom, boom.
Boom, boom, boom, boom.

Janeane Bostic-Metzel
Katlyn's Country Kids
York, PA

Smile o[...]

No doubt this Halloween [...]
with your little ones. If desir[...]
eyes and a nose on a pump[...]
student a smile cutout. Hav[...]
smile on their pumpkins. Th[...]
the rhyme, flipping the smile[...]
right side up when indicated[...]

Jack-o'-lantern, oh so brigh[...]
Felt so lonely one fall night.
His happy smile turned upsi[...]
And then he had a great big[...]

Jack-o'-lantern, oh so blue,
Met a friend and it is you!
His great big frown became [...]
And now he's happy once a[...]

Roxanne LaBell Dearman
Western NC Early Intervention [...]
    Are Deaf or Hard of Hearin[...]
Charlotte, NC

A Little Ice Cube

Here's an adorable ditty about an ice cube. Lead students in singing the song, encouraging them to dramatically melt to the floor throughout the last three lines.

(sung to the tune of "I'm a Little Teapot")

I'm a little ice cube,
Square and cold.
When I get warm
I'll melt, I'm told.
Look, here comes the sun!
This won't be fun.
Melting, melting—now I'm done!

Carolyn Elliott
Harrison-Hopedale Elementary
Hopedale, OH

Swimming Pool Supplies

What should little ones bring to the swimming pool? This song will help youngsters think of a few possibilities! Lead students in singing the first and second verses. Then repeat the second verse several times, each time substituting a different item to bring to the pool.

(sung to the tune of "The Mulberry Bush")

Here we go to the swimming pool,
The swimming pool, the swimming pool.
Here we go to the swimming pool
On this summer's day.

We'll bring [a friend] to the swimming pool,
The swimming pool, the swimming pool.
We'll bring [a friend] to the swimming pool
On this summer's day.

Continue with the following: *a float, a ball, a towel, sunscreen, a drink, flip-flops*

Kim Minafo
Apex, NC

BOOK UNITS

Chanting With Books

Youngsters are sure to enjoy these books based on traditional rhymes and the attention-grabbing activities that correspond with each selection.

ideas contributed by Ada Goren, Winston-Salem, NC

Five Little Monkeys Jumping on the Bed
Written and Illustrated by Eileen Christelow
Five little monkeys romp enthusiastically on a bed in this book fashioned after the classic rhyme.

A Classroom of Monkeys

Your little ones are the monkeys during this cute activity! Have youngsters help you count five students; then prompt the chosen children to stand in a row. Lead students in reciting the rhyme shown, inserting a child's name and prompting her to "fall" gracefully to the floor when indicated. Repeat the rhyme four more times, changing the numbers and inserting a different child's name each time, until all of the children are lying on the floor!

[Five] little children were jumping on the floor.
[Ellie] fell down, but there were [four] more.

Bandages for Bumps

All five of the monkeys in the book bumped only their heads, but this rhyme variation helps youngsters review a variety of body parts. Obtain a package of inexpensive adhesive bandages. Recite the rhyme shown, inserting a child's name. Have the child point to his elbow; then place a bandage on his elbow. Continue in the same way with other youngsters and body parts. Little ones will giggle at the bandages put on right over their clothing and are sure to talk about their patched-up parts all day long!

One day [Max] was jumping on the bed.
[He] fell off and bumped [his elbow].
Mama called the doctor and the doctor said,
"Put a bandage on that [elbow]!"

We're Going on a Bear Hunt
Written by Michael Rosen
Illustrated by Helen Oxenbury
A father and his children walk through swishy grass, a splashy river, and other noisy surroundings when they go on a bear hunt. Youngsters will particularly enjoy the humorous ending to this traditional chant.

A Book Hunt

Get youngsters excited about this fun read-aloud with a book hunt! In advance, tape a large paper star to the front cover of the book. Then hide the book in your classroom so that it's partially visible. Gather youngsters and explain that you have lost the book for storytime. Describe the star on the front of the book and then have youngsters conduct a search as you lead them in reciting the chant shown. When a child finds the book, rejoice with great enthusiasm and then have youngsters settle in for this read-aloud.

We're going on a book hunt.
We've got to find our book.
We want to have our storytime,
So look, look, look!

Fabulous Sound Effects

Make a rereading of the book extra special with sound effects! Gather six different instruments. (You might want to consider using everyday items that make noise, such as a container of rice or a ring of keys.) Give an instrument to each youngster and then tell each child which sound from the book his instrument will represent. For example, you might say that a tambourine will be the sound for the splashing water. Next, reread the book, prompting each child to play his instrument at the appropriate time. The end of the story is sure to be a symphony of sound! If desired, place the instruments and book at a center for further exploration.

159

Who Took the Cookies From the Cookie Jar?

Written by Bonnie Lass and Philemon Sturges
Illustrated by Ashley Wolff

When Skunk opens his cookie jar, he discovers that his cookies are missing! He checks with a variety of animal friends, but the cookies are nowhere to be found. In the end, it looks as if the ants are the culprits! No doubt little ones will ask for repeated readings of this classic chant.

Missing!

In advance, obtain an empty cookie jar and a class supply of cookies. Then place the cookies in a cupboard in your classroom. Tell students that you have brought a special treat. With great fanfare, open the cookie jar. Then act shocked that the jar is empty. Ask youngsters whether they know who took the cookies from the cookie jar. After students give several possible answers, present the book and tell them you will read it to see whether you can find out. Read aloud the story. Then explain that you remember seeing ants by the cupboard. Retrieve the cookies and then give youngsters a tasty snack.

Whose Cookie?

Youngsters get to know their classmates with this cute activity! Make a brown construction paper copy of the cookie pattern on page 161 for each child. Then personalize each cookie. Make a cookie for yourself as well and then place all the cookies in a cookie jar. Gather youngsters and lead them in reciting the rhyme shown. Have a child pull a cookie from the jar; then prompt the appropriate child to identify his cookie. Continue in the same way for each remaining cookie in the jar.

Who has a cookie in the cookie jar?
Whose name will we see?
Who has a cookie in the cookie jar?
Will it be you or me?

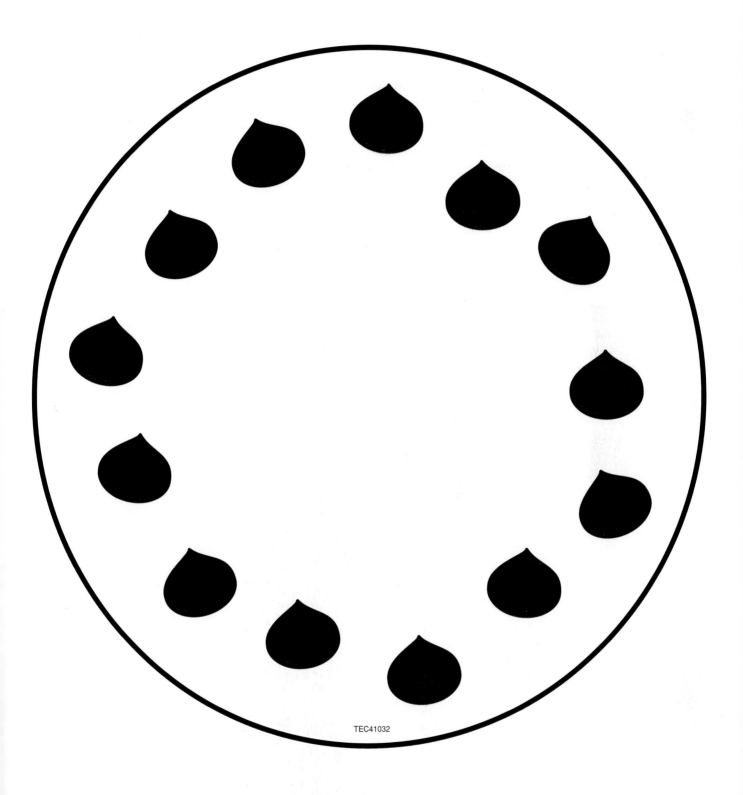

TEC41032

Lunch

Written and Illustrated by Denise Fleming

Join a ravenous rodent for his lunchtime romp through a buffet of colorful foods. Don't forget to look at the final page, where each food remnant clinging to the mouse's fur is labeled for a fun color review!

ideas by Ada Goren, Winston-Salem, NC

Ready for Lunch!
Promoting interest in a story

Get little ones excited about storytime with this prereading activity. Invite students to sit in a circle. As you hold up a paper plate, share with the group your favorite lunchtime food. Then pass the plate to the child beside you. After she names her favorite lunchtime food, invite her to pass the plate to the child beside her. Have youngsters continue to pass the plate around the circle until each child has had the opportunity to name her favorite lunchtime food. Then invite students to settle in as you read this tummy-tempting tale.

My favorite lunchtime food is pizza!

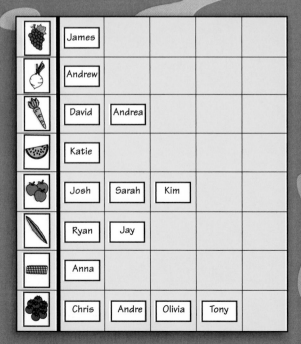

	James			
	Andrew			
	David	Andrea		
	Katie			
	Josh	Sarah	Kim	
	Ryan	Jay		
	Anna			
	Chris	Andre	Olivia	Tony

That Sounds Tasty!
Graphing

Mouse eats some foods that might sound tasty to your youngsters as well! Make a large graphing mat similar to the one shown. Color and cut out a copy of the food cards on page 164 and place one card in each row on the graph. Post the graph at student eye level. Help each child write his name on a sticky note. Then prompt him to choose his favorite food from the posted choices and attach his note to the appropriate row. Finally, discuss the results of the graph using words such as *more*, *less*, and *same*.

A Memorable Meal

Sequencing

Color and cut out a copy of the cards on page 164 and ready them for flannelboard use. Then place them in a lunch-size bag. Present the bag and explain that the mouse has packed his lunch for the day but can't remember in what order he likes to eat the items. Have students help remove the cards from the bag. Then have youngsters place the cards on the flannelboard in the same order the mouse eats the foods in the story. After all the cards have been sequenced, reread the story. As you read, invite a volunteer to remove each appropriate food and then place it back in the bag.

A Messy Mouse

Expressing oneself through arts and crafts

Youngsters decorate their own mouse with a variety of food options! Give each child a copy of the mouse reproducible on page 165. Have each child think of a food and its color. Then prompt her to use a cotton swab and paint in a corresponding color to paint dots on the mouse. Encourage her to continue in the same way with several other colors. Then have the child name her chosen foods as you label each paint color. When the projects are dry, display them with a title such as "Hungry Mice!"

What's for Lunch?

Participating in a song

Ask a child to name a different kind of food the mouse might like to have for lunch. Then lead little ones in singing the song shown, substituting the name of the food when appropriate. Continue in the same way, with a different youngster suggesting the food each time.

(sung to the tune of "If You're Happy and You Know It")

Oh, the mouse will eat [spaghetti] for his lunch.
Oh, the mouse will eat [spaghetti] for his lunch.
With a smack and then a slurp
And a tiny mousy burp,
Oh, the mouse will eat [spaghetti] for his lunch!

Welcome-to-School Centers

Welcome youngsters to school with hands-on centers that are just perfect for the beginning of the school year!

Family Connection

Puzzle Center

In advance, ask each child's parent to send a family photo to school. Make an enlarged copy of each photo; then laminate each copy and return the original photo to the family. Puzzle-cut each copy into five or six pieces. Store each puzzle in a resealable plastic bag labeled with the child's name and then place the bags at a center. After a child removes his puzzle pieces from the bag, he puts together his family photo. *(For a variation on this activity, see "Photo Puzzles" on page 81.)*

Christine Vohs
Blue Valley Montessori
Overland Park, KS

Fabric Match

Math Center

To prepare for this center, obtain fabric scraps in a variety of colors and patterns. Use pinking shears (to help prevent fraying) to cut squares from the fabric. Place the fabric squares at a center. A visiting child looks for fabric squares that match and places them together. For an added challenge for students who are ready, create simple patterns with the squares for each child to copy or extend.

Bonnie Lanterman
St. Charles, MO

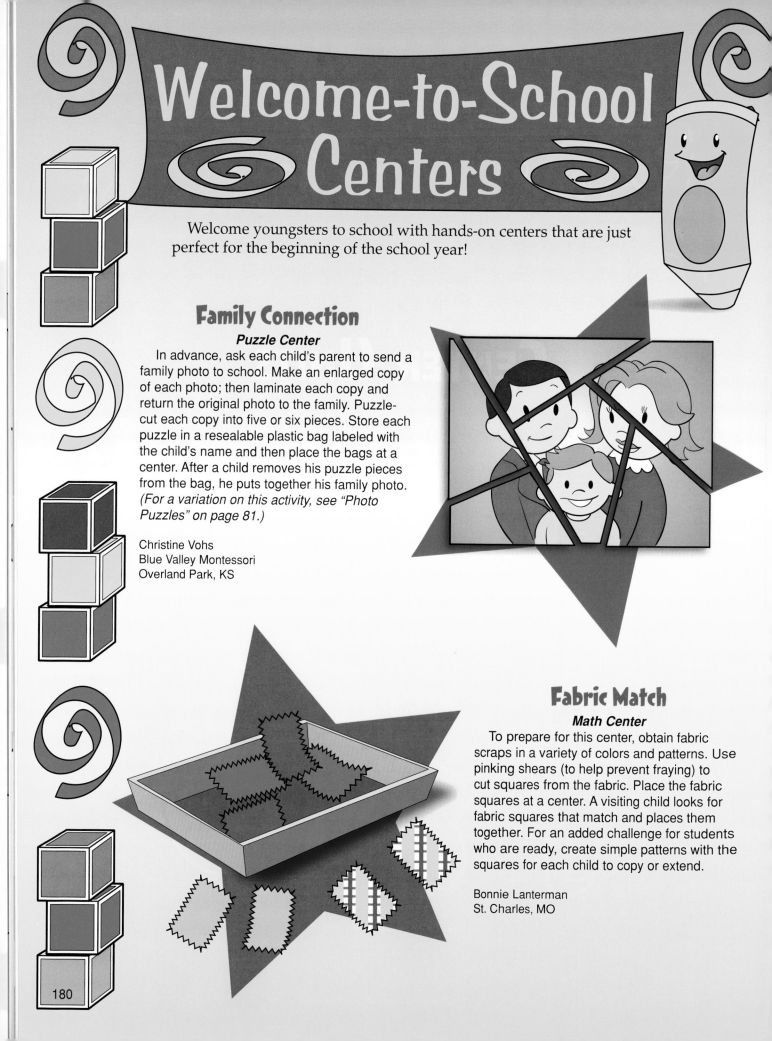

Cookie-Cutter Names

Literacy Center

Trace each child's name onto a card stock strip using alphabet cookie cutters. Laminate the cards to provide a nonstick surface. Place the cards, a set of alphabet cookie cutters, and play dough at a table. A youngster visits the center and uses the cookie cutters and play dough to make each letter in her name. Then she places each play dough letter atop the matching letter on her name card.

Christine Vohs
Blue Valley Montessori
Overland Park, KS

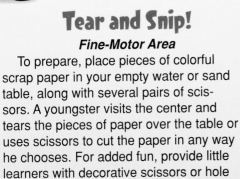

Photo Copies

Flannelboard Center

Use the patterns on page 183 to make several felt cutouts in a variety of colors. Add details to the cutouts with permanent marker. Choose some cutouts and arrange them on your flannelboard in a desired fashion. Then take a photo of the flannelboard. Continue in the same way with other felt pieces until you have several photographs. Then place the photos and cutouts near your flannelboard. A child chooses a photo and uses the cutouts to re-create what she sees. She repeats the process with other photos.

Camille Cooper
Emporia State University for Early Childhood Education
Emporia, KS

Tear and Snip!

Fine-Motor Area

To prepare, place pieces of colorful scrap paper in your empty water or sand table, along with several pairs of scissors. A youngster visits the center and tears the pieces of paper over the table or uses scissors to cut the paper in any way he chooses. For added fun, provide little learners with decorative scissors or hole punchers as well.

Stacee Buskirk
South Penn Elementary
Cumberland, MD

181

On Our Way to School!

Game Center

To make a gameboard, mount a photograph of each child on a separate house cutout and then mount the houses on a sheet of poster board. Add a "Start" space, a school cutout for the finish, and the other details shown. Then place the gameboard at a center along with four toy cars in different colors and a large die. Invite four children to the center. Each student chooses a car and places it on Start. Then each youngster, in turn, rolls the die, counts the dots, and moves his car over the corresponding number of houses. Play continues until each player arrives at the school.

Janis Dirnbeck and Robyn Christopher
Point Elementary
St. Louis, MO

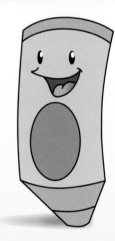

Texture Table

Sensory Center

Collect a variety of textured items, such as sandpaper, cellophane, corrugated cardboard, bubble wrap, velvet, corduroy, and tweed. Secure the items to a tabletop with double-sided tape. Invite a child to visit the center and run his hands over the tabletop to feel the assorted textures. Encourage him to use words to describe how each texture feels. When it's time for a change, remove the textured items and replace them with new ones!

Peggy Wieck
Litchfield Prekindergarten
Litchfield, IL

TEC41032

TEC41032

TEC41032

TEC41032

TEC41032

Slightly Spooky Centers

Spiders, jack-o'-lanterns, and squishy green goo! Your youngsters are sure to think these centers are a scream.

ideas contributed by Ada Goren
Winston-Salem, NC

Happy Hayride
Fine-Motor Area

Little ones get a fine-motor workout adding details to a hayride! Have each child color a copy of page 187. Then invite her to use a pair of scissors to snip scraps of yellow construction paper into small strips. Next, have her brush glue above the wagon and press the strips into the glue. What a fun hayride!

Squishy Green Goo
Sensory Center

To prepare, place in a heavy-duty resealable bag the following ingredients: 5 tablespoons of cornstarch, ½ cup of water, ½ cup of vegetable oil, and several drops of green food coloring. Seal the bag; then fold over the top of the bag and reinforce the opening with clear packing tape. Place the bag at a table. A child pushes and manipulates the bag to observe how the squishy, gooey ingredients combine and separate. What fun!

Keely Peasner
Liberty Ridge Head Start
Bonney Lake, WA

Itsy-Bitsy Spider

Music Center

Spotlight this popular song with student-made props! Make a class supply of the house pattern on page 188. Place the houses at a table along with a class supply of bendable straws and plastic spider rings. Quietly play a recording of the traditional song "The Itsy-Bitsy Spider" at the center. A child colors a house; then he slides a spider ring onto a straw and tapes the straw to the house to resemble a water-spout. The child sings along with the recording and moves the spider up and down the spout to reflect the lyrics.

Donna Pulley, New Heights Preschool, Phoenix, AZ

Slimy Bugs

Snack Center

Delight students with this fun and simple snack! Mix several drops of green food coloring with vanilla or white chocolate pudding to make slime. Place a supply of Keebler Grahams Bug Bites crackers in a bowl. A child places a dollop of pudding on a plate along with a scoop of the graham crackers. Then he dips his bugs into the slime before gobbling them up. Mmmm—tasty!

Toothy Grins

Math Center

Youngsters practice counting to give these jack-o'-lanterns great big toothy grins! Enlarge the pumpkin pattern on page 189; then make two orange construction paper copies. Cut facial features from each pumpkin, omitting the teeth; then color the stems green and mount the pumpkins on yellow construction paper. Place the resulting jack-o'-lanterns at a table along with a jumbo die and orange paper squares (teeth). Two youngsters visit the center. One child rolls the die and places the corresponding number of teeth on a pumpkin. His partner repeats the process with the second pumpkin. Then the children compare the pumpkins, using words such as *more, less,* or *same.*

Leslie Seabase, Saginaw Chippewwa Academy, Mt. Pleasant, MI

Let's Be Frank

Craft Center

Gather the supplies below for each child and then place the supplies in your craft center. Invite youngsters to the center and help them follow the directions below to complete this "spook-tacular" Halloween lantern.

Materials for one lantern:

12" x 18" green construction paper,   scissors
    folded and programmed as shown   glue
3" x 18" black construction paper strip   black marker
white construction paper eyes   stapler
gray construction paper bolts   tape
green construction paper handle

Directions:

Cut along the preprogrammed lines as shown; then unfold the paper and lay it flat on a tabletop. Trim one side of the black strip with a zigzag cut. Then glue the strip to the green paper to make hair. Draw pupils on the eyes and glue them below the hair. Then draw a mouth below the eyes. When the glue is dry, roll the paper and staple it in place. Tape a bolt to each side of the project and staple the handle to the project as shown.

Bonnie Martin, Hopewell Country Day School, Pennington, NJ

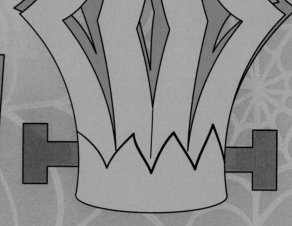

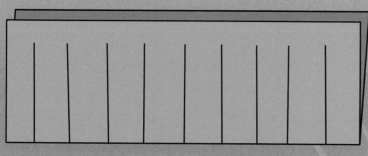

M Is for Mummy

Literacy Center

This cute letter craft is "mmmmarvelous"! Make a gray construction paper *M* cutout for each youngster. Then place the *M*s at a table along with lengths of white crepe paper streamers and glue. Have a child visit the center and take an *M*. Then encourage her to identify the letter and its sound. Have her glue streamer pieces to the letter to resemble a mummy. Then help her trim any streamers hanging over the edge of the letter. Finally, have her glue construction paper eyes to the project.

Heather Lionetti, The Academy, Middletown, NJ

Note to the teacher: Use with "Happy Hayride" on page 184.

House Pattern
Use with "Itsy-Bitsy Spider" on page 185.

TEC41033

TEC41033

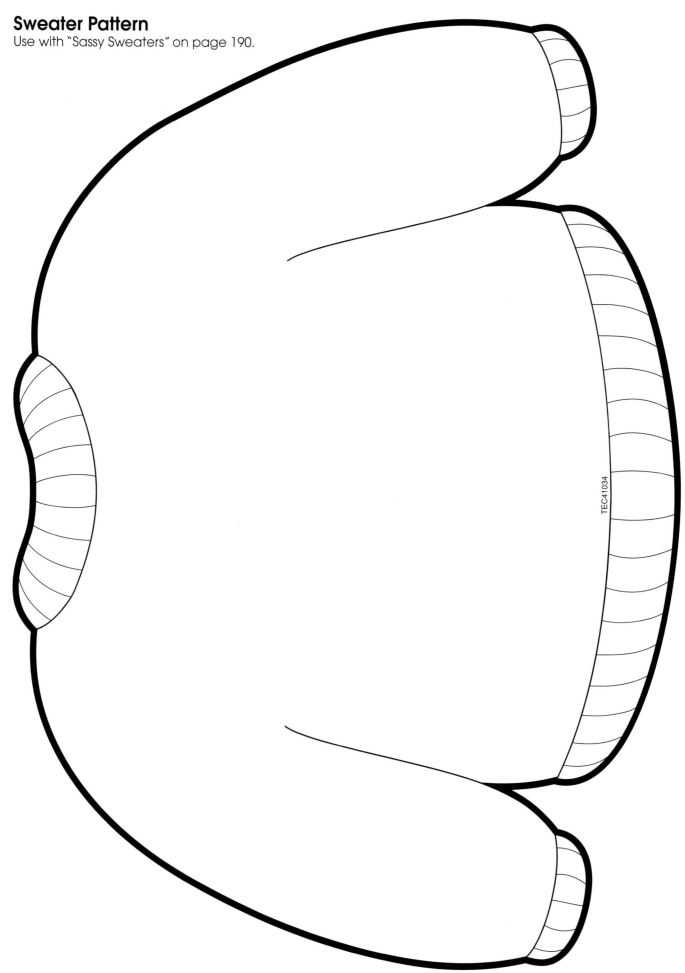

TEC41034

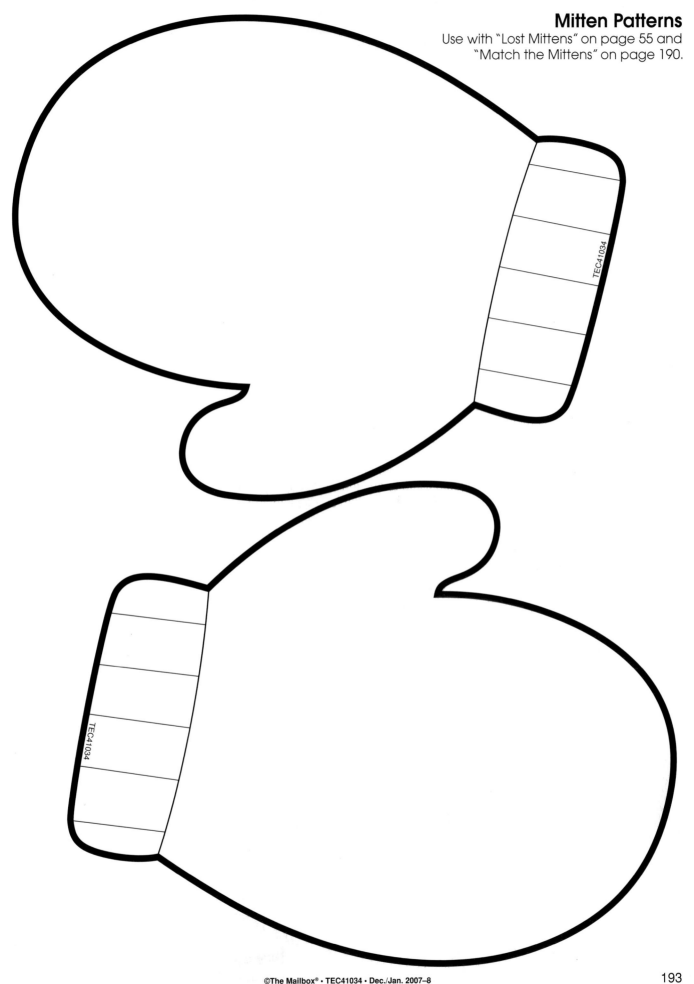

Mitten Patterns
Use with "Lost Mittens" on page 55 and
"Match the Mittens" on page 190.

TEC41034

TEC41034

A Lovely Selection of Centers

Youngsters are sure to fall in love
with this adorable collection of centers.

ideas contributed by Lucia Kemp Henry
Fallon, NV

Royal Crowns
Math Center

Youngsters practice patterning while creating these regal headbands! In advance, die-cut a supply of construction paper hearts from two contrasting colors of paper. Attach some of the hearts to a construction paper headband in an AB pattern. Then place this sample at a table along with the remaining hearts and a class supply of headbands. A youngster visits the center and glues hearts to a headband in an AB pattern, using the sample as a guide. Then she decorates each heart with sequins as desired. After the glue is dry, size each headband appropriately.

A Lovely Tree
Art Center

Cut from brown bulletin board paper a large tree shape, minus foliage, and mount it on a wall. Cut out a supply of red and pink construction paper hearts and place them at your art center along with scissors; glue; and an assortment of collage items, such as curling ribbon, pom-poms, sequins, glitter, and Valentine's Day stickers. Invite a child to visit the center and use the craft materials to decorate a heart as desired. Mount the projects to the tree. Then attach pink construction paper bird cutouts (patterns on page 196) to the display.

194

Broken Hearts
Literacy Center

To prepare, use a permanent marker to write a different letter on each of several craft foam hearts. Then cut each heart in half vertically with a different puzzle cut. Place the hearts at a center. A visiting child fits two matching heart halves together and then identifies the letter. She continues in the same way until she has "mended" all the broken hearts!

Laura Canavan, Chestnut Children's Center, Needham, MA

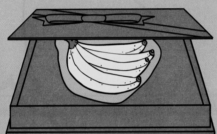

I ate all the candy...

...so for Valentine's Day, I'm giving you a box of <u>bananas</u> instead!

Valentine Surprise!
Writing Center

This sweet valentine box holds an unexpected surprise! Give each child a red or pink copy of page 197. Have him cut out the patterns and then glue the box bottom to a sheet of construction paper programmed with the words shown. Next, have him choose a random item from a grocery store circular. Encourage him to cut out the picture and glue it to the box bottom. Then staple the box top to the bottom where indicated. Encourage him to identify the picture as you write its name in the blank space. Now that's a Valentine's Day surprise!

Sweet Cookie Sort
Play Dough Center

To prepare for this center, mix red glitter into a batch of pink play dough. Make two red construction paper heart cutouts in different sizes; then laminate each heart. Place the play dough at a center along with several rolling pins and heart-shaped cookie cutters in two different sizes. A child visits the center and uses the props to make Valentine's Day cookies. Then she places each cookie on the corresponding heart. What a yummy-looking display!

195

Exploring the Senses in Centers

Little ones explore the five senses with this selection of splendid centers!

ideas contributed by Ada Goren, Winston-Salem, NC

See the Match
Puzzle Center

To prepare for this center, enlarge several photographs of different classroom objects and laminate them for durability. Puzzle-cut each photo and then store each puzzle in a separate resealable plastic bag. Place the puzzles at a center. A youngster visits the center, removes the puzzle pieces from a bag, and then assembles the puzzle. After the puzzle is complete, he uses his sense of sight to scan the room and find the item pictured in the puzzle.

Marvelous Minty Smell
Art Center

This project smells good enough to eat! Mix together equal amounts of nonmentholated shaving cream and glue. Add green food coloring and mint extract to the mixture. Place cone cutouts at your art center along with construction paper, plastic spoons, black hole-punched dots, and glue. A child glues a cone to a sheet of paper. She spoons a few dollops of the mixture above the cone and then spreads it as desired. Finally, she sprinkles black dots on the ice cream scoop so they resemble chocolate chips.

Mint Extract

Sam

Lovely Lemon Scent

Water Table

Fill your water table with warm water and lemon-scented liquid dish detergent. (If desired, add a bit of lemon extract for an even stronger scent.) Then add dishware from your housekeeping center along with several sponges. Place a tub of rinse water, a dish rack, and a few dish towels nearby. Encourage visiting young-sters to sniff the lemon-fresh scent as they scrub the dishes sparkling clean!

Whipped Cream Cheese

See and Taste

Snack Center

Place at a table a bowl of whipped cream cheese, craft sticks, food coloring, paper plates, and minibagel halves. Give a visiting child a dollop of cream cheese and invite her to taste it. Next, encourage her to use a craft stick to mix a few drops of food coloring with her cream cheese. Have her taste the cream cheese again to determine if the food coloring changed the flavor. Finally, invite her to spread the colorful cream cheese onto a bagel half and then eat her yummy treat!

Tool Touch

Math Center

To prepare for this tactile center, gather pairs of familiar school tools, such as glue bottles, markers, crayons, glue sticks, and rulers. Place one item from each pair in a separate clean sock and secure the opening closed with a rubber band. Place the socks and the remaining tools at a center. A youngster visits the center, selects a tool, and then feels each sock to find its match. After he decides a match has been made, he places the pair to the side. He repeats the process with each remaining tool.

Janet Boyce, Cokato, MN

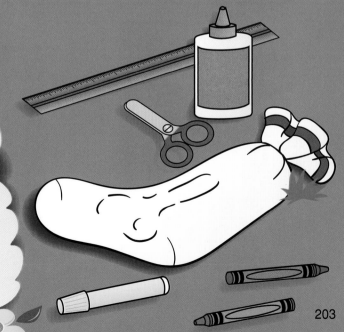

Scented Letter Match

Literacy Center

Strengthen your little ones' sense of smell with this aromatic idea! Make several small batches of play dough. Add a different scented oil—such as peppermint, cinnamon, apple, or rose—to each batch. Add scents to cotton balls to match the play dough and then glue them to separate sheets of laminated tagboard. Place the scented cotton balls and play dough at a table along with alphabet cookie cutters. A child visits the center and uses a cookie cutter to make a scented letter. She identifies the letter, smells it, and then places it on the tagboard with the corresponding cotton ball. She continues in the same way with other letters and play dough scents.

Mary Robles, Portland, OR

Tap, Squeak, and Rattle!

Sensory Center

Youngsters need their listening ears for this partner activity! To prepare, gather several familiar items that each make a sound, such as a baby rattle, a squeeze toy, a bell, and a plastic hammer. Place the items at a table. Two children visit the center, examine the items, and listen to the sounds the items make. Then one child turns his back and becomes the listener. His partner uses one of the items to make a sound; then the listener names the item. Play continues in the same manner with each remaining item; then the partners switch places.

LITERACY UNITS

Fire Prevention

Little ones learn about fire safety with these red-hot literacy ideas!

All About Firefighters

Making connections between spoken and written words

Encourage youngsters to put on their thinking caps to help you complete this rebus poem! In advance, color and cut out a copy of the cards on page 213. Write on chart paper the poem shown and place the cards in plain view. Have youngsters identify the pictures on the cards. Then read aloud the first line of the poem. Invite a volunteer to choose the picture she thinks belongs in the line. Then reread the sentence using the chosen card. After confirming a correct choice, have her attach the card to the corresponding line. Continue in the same manner until the poem is complete. Then read aloud the finished poem.

Tricia Brown, Bowling Green, KY

A firefighter puts a 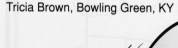 on his head.
He puts heavy ___ on his feet.
He drives a _____ all around town.
I think that is really quite neat!
A firefighter wears special _____
   on his hands
And puts a ____ on too.
He is a hero every day,
Helping people like me and you.
A firefighter puts out a _____
With a special ____ that sprays.
He may even have a pet ____ .
I could be a _____ one day.

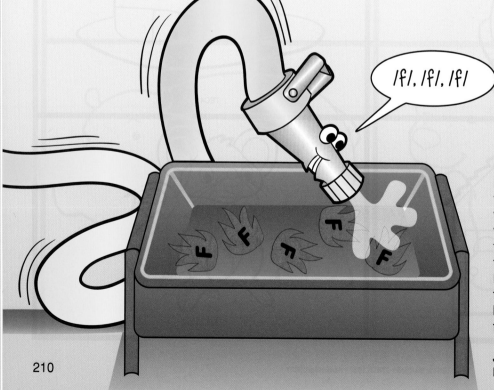

/f/, /f/, /f/

Fire and Water

Developing an awareness of letters and sounds

To prepare, cut out several flame shapes from red craft foam. Use a permanent marker to label each shape with the letter *F.* Float the flames in your water table and place spray bottles filled with water nearby. Invite your little firefighters to use the spray bottles to squirt the fire. To reinforce the sound of the letter *F,* encourage each child to make the /f/ sound each time he squirts the bottle. If desired, provide firefighter hats for added fun!

Joanne Sabbagh, Prime Time Preschool Lincoln, RI

Stop, Drop, and Roll!

Listening for understanding

To prepare for this activity, make a fire prop by taping lengths of red and orange crepe paper to a cardboard tube. As part of your fire safety unit, talk to students about the importance of knowing how to stop, drop, and roll in case their clothes were to catch fire. Help youngsters understand that it is important not to run because it will make the fire spread. Show youngsters how to stop, lie on the ground, and roll back and forth. Then, in turn, wiggle the fire prop near each student and encourage her to demonstrate how to stop, drop, and roll.

Patricia Wolf, Kids Cozy Corners, Hartford, WI

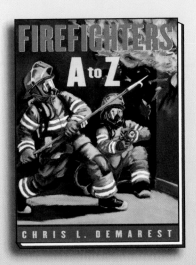

Jump in the fire truck; off we go!

Hurry to get there; don't go slow!

Turn on the siren—woo, woo, woo!

The fire truck is coming through!

On the Way!

Tracking print from left to right

Make a class supply of firefighter pointers similar to the one shown (use the firefighter card on page 213). Also make a class supply of page 214. (Be sure to have a copy of the page and a pointer for yourself!) Display the page and have youngsters watch as you read the words, following the text from left to right with your pointer. Then give each child a copy of the page and a pointer. Read each line aloud and encourage little ones to follow the words from the fire truck to the fire using their pointers.

Tricia Brown, Bowling Green, KY

Fighting Fires From A to Z

Matching letters

Obtain a copy of the book *Firefighters A to Z* by Chris L. Demarest, along with a set of alphabet cards and a firefighter hat. Prior to a second reading of the book, give an alphabet card to each child and place any remaining cards faceup on the floor. Place the hat upside down near the cards. Read aloud the first page of the book, pointing to the letter. Encourage the child with the matching letter to hold his card in the air. After confirming a correct match, invite him to place his card in the hat. If no one has the matching card, ask a volunteer to look for it among the remaining cards. Continue in the same manner until all the cards have been placed in the hat.

Tricia Brown

Hot Topic!

Making connections between spoken and written words

Get little ones talking about what fire means to them with this activity! For each child, trim a sheet of white construction paper so it resembles flames. Have her glue red and yellow cellophane squares to the flames. Then trim the edges as needed. Next, ask each youngster to tell you something she knows about fire; then record her response on a construction paper strip. After the projects are dry, attach each child's dictation to her flames and refer to them to discuss fire safety.

Jana Sanderson, Rainbow School, Stockton, CA
Paula Glass, Foundations Christian Academy, Oklahoma City, OK

Fire is hot!   —Emily

Five Firefighters

Participating in a song

Your little firefighters will be eager to participate in this flannelboard activity! To prepare, cut out five copies of the firefighter card on page 213 and ready the cards for flannelboard use. Lead youngsters in singing four verses of the song shown, having a child add a card to the flannelboard for each verse and increasing the number as appropriate. Have students finish the song by singing the final verse and adding the fifth card to the flannelboard.

Five Firefighters
(sung to the tune of "Five Little Ducks")

[One] firefighter(s) went out to spray
Water on a flame one day.
It was such an enormous fire;
[She] called for another firefighter.

Final verse:
Five firefighters went out to spray
Water on a flame one day.
They sprayed the water till the fire was out.
Their work was done; we heard them shout! (Hooray!)

adapted from an idea by Jana Sanderson

Fire Prevention Cards

Use with "All About Firefighters" on page 210. Use the firefighter card with "On the Way!" on page 211 and "Five Firefighters" on page 212.

TEC41033

TEC41033

TEC41033

TEC41033

TEC41033

TEC41033

TEC41033

TEC41033

TEC41033

Jump in the fire truck; off we go!

Hurry to get there; don't go slow!

Turn on the siren—woo, woo, woo, woo!

The fire truck is coming through!

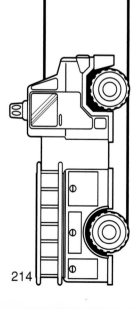

214

©The Mailbox® • TEC41033 • Oct./Nov. 2007

Note to the teacher: Use with "On the Way!" on page 211.

A FLURRY of Class Book Ideas

Here's a selection of class book ideas and tips that "snow-body" can resist!

Knock, Knock!

Who's at the door? No doubt youngsters will be eager to tell you with this lift-the-flap book! Program a class supply of 9" x 12" construction paper with the words shown at the top of the page. Then have each child color and cut out a copy of the door pattern on page 219. Help her tape her door to the programmed paper so that it can be opened as if it were a real door. After asking the youngster who might be at the door, write her words under the door and have her draw a matching picture above the words. Bind all the finished projects behind a cover titled "Knock, Knock! Who's There?" Then read the book aloud with your youngsters, prompting them to chant the repetitive words together.

Deborah Ryan, Early Head Start, Milwaukie, OR

Knock, knock!
Who's there?

It's my mom!

Beautiful Colors!

This book grows throughout your students' study of different colors. Gather a 12" x 18" sheet of tagboard to match the color your students are currently studying and label it with the appropriate color word. Place the tagboard at a table along with glue sticks, scissors, and magazines. Invite students to cut from the magazines pictures that match the color and then glue the pictures to the tagboard. When the tagboard is full, laminate it for durability. Then attach metal rings to the tagboard. Place a sheet of tagboard in a different color at the center and repeat the process, attaching the finished laminated page to the rings with the previous page. Continue in the same way for each color in your color study. Your little ones will love to watch this book grow!

Melissa Burke, Heritage Christian Academy, Manvel, TX
Kimberly Taylor, Hawley Youth Organization, Syracuse, NY

green

My Hands Can!

Youngsters' hands can do so many things! Have each child make colorful handprints on a sheet of construction paper programmed with the prompt "My hands can…" Then take a photograph of each child throughout the school day as he completes a task that uses his hands, such as building, stirring, scooping, or climbing. Attach each child's photo to his handprints. Then help the youngster complete his prompt. Laminate the finished pages for durability and then bind them behind a cover titled "My Hands Can…"

Missy Goldenberg, Beth Shalom Nursery School
Overland Park, KS

My hands can...
build with blocks!

Durable Covers

Vinyl placemats make simple seasonal covers for class books! Stack two identical placemats and punch holes along the left-hand side. Hole-punch your pages in the same way. Then sandwich the pages between the placemats and bind the stack together with metal rings.

Ronna Decarli-Lott, Portville Elementary
Portville, NY

What Was That?

Little ones use their imaginations for this adorable idea! Program a sheet of paper with "Grrr! What was that?" Then make a copy for each child. Have each student name and describe what might be making the noise. Then write his words on the back of the paper and have him draw a picture above the words. Stack the finished pages under a cover titled "Grrr! What Was That?" You may wish to make similar class books titled "Squeak! What Was That?" or "Screech! What Was That?"

Deborah Ryan, Early Head Start, Milwaukie, OR

Grrr! What was that?

It was a lion!

Mixed-Up Names

Attach each child's photo to a nine-inch square piece of construction paper. Then write each child's name on a 3" x 9" strip of construction paper. Gather two 9" x 12" sheets of construction paper to make a front and back cover. Then bind the photos at the top of the book and the names at the bottom of the book, as shown, making sure that the names and photos are not in the same order. Youngsters will enjoy flipping through the book to match the names to the photos!

Deb Jacox, Busy Bees Preschool, Lincoln, NE

Thomas

Take-Home Tips

At the end of the year, dismantle all your class books and then sort the pages into piles based on the child's name. Bind each student's pages together for her to take home. Another option is to place the name of each class book in a bag and then have each child draw a name and take home the corresponding book to keep.

Melissa Burke, Heritage Christian Academy, Manvel, TX
Keri Meyer, Garrett's Way, Newtown Square, PA

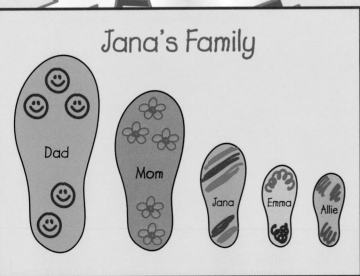

Jana's Family

Dad

Mom

Jana

Emma

Allie

Funny Feet

Send home with each youngster construction paper and instructions prompting each family member to trace one of his feet and then cut out the foot, decorate it, and label it with his name. When each student brings the foot cutouts back to school, help her glue the cutouts to a sheet of construction paper programmed similar to the one shown. Bind the finished pages together along with a cover titled "Funny Family Feet."

Linda Thomas and Debby Wright, Canterbury School, Fort Myers, FL
Cynthia Thurman, Montezuma Elementary, Stockton, CA

Drew

Snow is on the cat.

Snow Everywhere!

This class book is particularly fun to make after a big snowfall! Have children notice how snow covers everything, from the trees and bushes to cars in the parking lot. Encourage each child to draw a picture on light-colored construction paper of something that could possibly get covered with snow. Next, have him spread glue over the drawing with a glue stick and then dab a cotton ball over the glue. Wispy bits of cotton ball will stick to the glue, giving the object a snow-covered appearance. Write a sentence below the drawing similar to the one shown. Then bind the pages together with a cover titled "Snow Everywhere!"

Lois Otten, Kingdom Kids Preschool, Sheboygan, WI

I Don't Like It!

Here's a book that's sure to cause oodles of giggles! Give each child a copy of page 220 and encourage him to draw a picture of something he doesn't like in the space on the paper. Write the name of the child and the object or activity in the appropriate blanks. Then help the student glue his page to a 9" x 12" sheet of construction paper. Laminate the pages if desired. Then bind the pages together with a cover titled "I Don't Like It!"

Deborah Ryan, Early Head Start, Milwaukie, OR

Derek doesn't like taking a bath.

Not one little bit!

ABCs and 123s

To make a fun and engaging alphabet book, take a photo of each child holding, wearing, or standing next to an object that begins with a different letter of the alphabet. Have each child glue heer photo to a sheet of construction paper labeled with the corresponding letter. Then bind the pages together with a cover.

To make a similar number book, have each child count a different number of common classroom objects. Then take each child's photograph next to the objects. Have each child glue his photo to a page programmed with a sentence similar to the one shown. Then bind the pages together with a cover.

Sandra Bendickson, The Salvation Army Child Care Center, Peoria, IL
Amy Cleeton, Okaw Valley Intermediate, Findlay, IL

Uu

3

Ethan found 3 cars.

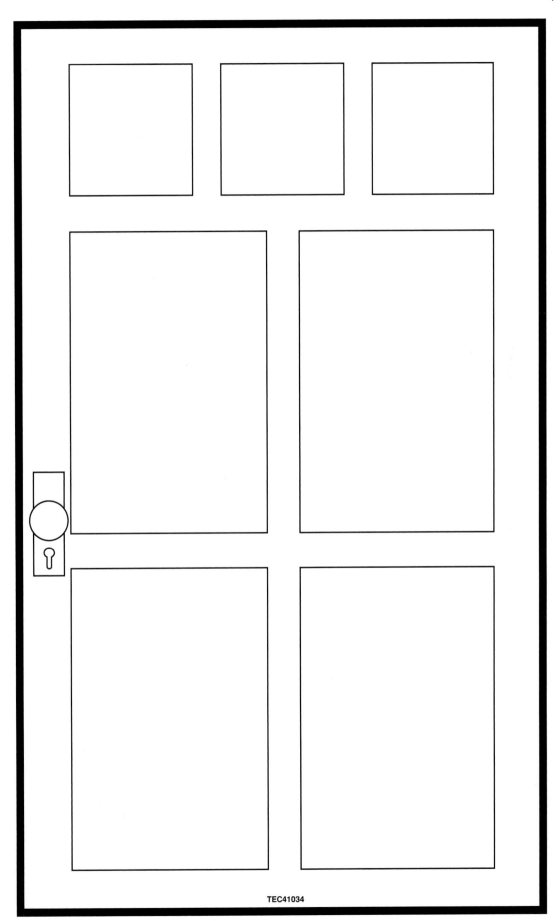

TEC41034

_____ doesn't like

_____.

Not one little bit!

Fun With Opposites

Little ones are sure to enjoy this engaging collection of opposites activities!

There's That Shadow!

Little ones get plenty of practice using the opposites *in* and *out* with this adorable idea! In advance, cut a hole in the bottom of each filter in a class supply of brown cone-style coffee filters. (Be sure to prepare one for yourself!) Have each child color a groundhog cutout (pattern on page 224) and then tape it to a drinking straw. Next, have her put the straw through the hole in a filter and pull the groundhog inside. Then lead youngsters in reciting the poem shown, encouraging each child to move her groundhog in and out of its hole at the appropriate times.

If I were a groundhog sleeping in my house,
All day long I'd be as quiet as a mouse.
But on Groundhog Day, I would jump right out.
"Oops! There's my shadow!" I would shout.
I'd run into my house and shiver with fear.
"Sorry, folks! See you next year!"

Jeanie Young, Lake Orion Community Schools, Lake Orion, MI
Dawn Fuchs, The Learning Nest, Mt. Freedom, NJ

Wash Day

Hang a makeshift clothesline in your outdoor area and fill two tubs with warm water. Add a little laundry soap to one tub, and set a basket of doll clothes and a container of spring-style clothespins nearby. Have students feel the clothes to determine that they are dry. Then invite youngsters to help wash and rinse the clothes, reinforcing that the opposite of *dry* is *wet*. When the scrubbing is done, have little ones hang the clothes on the clothesline to dry. As students manipulate the clothespins, reinforce that the opposite of *open* is *close*.

Kimberly Torson
Dearborn West UAW-Ford Family Service and
    Learning Center Child Development Center
Dearborn, MI

221

The Opposites Cheer!

Here's an engaging way to introduce or reinforce opposites with your little ones! Motivate youngsters to join you by chanting the introductory verse shown. Then lead students in chanting the call-and-response verse, prompting them to respond with the words in parentheses. Extend the call-and-response portion with additional opposites. Then chant the final verse to conclude the activity.

Hey, everybody,
Come over here!
It's time to do
The Opposites Cheer!

I'll say [hot]! You say [cold]!
[Hot]! [(Cold)]! [Hot]! [(Cold)]!

Thanks, everybody,
For joining me here
To help me with
The Opposites Cheer!

Amy Countiss
Washington-Jackson Elementary
Wichita Falls, TX

Border Bands

Recycle scraps of bulletin board border to help teach little ones the opposites *left* and *right!* Gather two scraps of bulletin board border in different colors for each child. Help each student use a permanent marker to label one piece of border with *L*s and the remaining piece of border with *R*s. Size each piece of border to the appropriate wrist and then tape them in place to make bracelets. After reinforcing that left is the opposite of right, engage students in a lively round of the Hokey-Pokey!

Tina Borek
Pulaski, TN

222

Dirty and Clean

What's the opposite of *dirty?* Why, it's *clean,* of course! Reinforce this opposite pair with the help of a double-sided stick puppet. Give each child two pink construction paper pig head cutouts (pattern on page 224). Help him glue the pigs back-to-back, with a jumbo craft stick between them. Then instruct him to lightly pat brown fingerpaint on one pig so it resembles mud. When the puppets are dry, lead youngsters in singing the song shown, directing them to turn their puppets around at the appropriate time.

(sung to the tune of "I'm a Little Teapot")

I'm a pig who's dirty—I will play
In the cool, wet mud all day.
But I have a friend who's clean and neat.
She takes baths and smells so sweet!

Gina Glenn
Fish Hawk Early Learning Center
Lithia, FL

Opposites Book

Have students illustrate a class book of opposites with real-life photographs! To make a book, take photographs of students acting out opposites; for example, take photos of one child standing and one sitting, one child with eyes open and one with eyes closed, or one child with shoes on and one with shoes off. Mount each pair of photographs on paper. Then enlist youngsters' help in labeling the photographs. Bind the finished pages together. Use this book at circle time or in a center for opposites reinforcement!

Mary Zalabak
Marycare Child Care
Bolingbrook, IL

stand   sit

Groundhog Pattern
Use with "Groundhog's Shadow" on page 59 and "There's That Shadow!" on page 221.

TEC41035

Pig Head Pattern
Use with "Dirty and Clean" on page 223.

TEC41035

Letters and Sounds

Super Letter Center

Help little ones practice letter recognition and formation at this super center! Obtain a trifold presentation board (or fold cardboard to make a presentation board) and then attach to the board copies of your featured letter and a picture of an animal or object whose name begins with the corresponding letter sound. Place the board at a center along with items such as those shown to help little ones practice forming and recognizing the letter.

Cathy Germino, A Little Folks School House
Manchester, NH

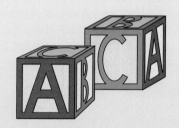

Plunger *O* Placemat

Youngsters are sure to remember the letter *O* with this cute activity! Have youngsters press an unused rubber sink plunger in a pan of paint and then press the plunger on a sheet of paper several times to make a letter *O* placemat. Allow the paint to dry. Then, while students are out of the classroom, place each placemat at the corresponding youngster's seat along with a plate holding a mini doughnut and O-shaped cereal. When students come back to the room, explain that Mr. O came to visit and left special treats in the shape of the letter *O!* Then have little ones nibble on their treats.

Becky Edwards, South Roebuck Baptist Child Development Center,
 Birmingham, AL
Monica Saunders, Hazelwild, Fredericksburg, VA

2225

The Sandwich Game

Label each side of a cube-shaped box with a different letter, making sure that three sides are labeled with the letter *S*. Cut craft foam to make two bread slice cutouts and a class supply of sandwich topping cutouts. Place a bread slice on the floor. Have a child roll the cube and identify the letter. If the letter is an *S*, she places one of the toppings on the bread. If the letter is not an *S*, she identifies the letter and then rolls again. Continue until each child has had a chance to add a topping. Then place the final slice of bread on the stack of toppings and have youngsters enthusiastically yell, "Sandwich!"

Cross It Out

Give each child a crayon and a clipboard with a sheet of paper labeled with six different letters. Dim the lights slightly, locate one of the letters on materials posted around your room, and then shine a flashlight on the letter. Have students name the letter and then cross out the matching letter on their sheets. Repeat the process for each remaining letter.

Katherine Bryan, T.C.O.C. Head Start, Streator, IL

Choose and Sing

Scatter letter cards in your large-group area. Then gather students around the cards. Encourage a child to choose and name a letter. Lead youngsters in singing the song shown, substituting the child's name, the letter name, and the letter sound where indicated. Have the child place the letter in a separate pile. Then continue in the same way with different youngsters.

(sung to the tune of "He's Got the Whole World in His Hands")

[Sam]'s got the letter [*M*] in his hand.
[Sam]'s got the letter [*M*] in his hand.
[Sam]'s got the letter [*M*] in his hand.
[/m/, /m/, /m/, /m/, /m/, /m/, /m/, /m/].

Cathy Seibel, Greensburg, PA

Bear's Belly

What has this bear been eating? Why, it's been eating things that begin with /b/! Make a large bear cutout and attach it to a wall. Then color and cut out the cards on page 228 and place them on a table. Have a child choose a card and then name the picture. Have the remaining students identify whether the name begins with /b/. If it does, help the child attach the card to the bear's tummy. Continue in the same way for each remaining card.

Lottie Hart, Miss Kathy's Early Learning Center, Pensacola, FL

A Stolen Letter

Ready letter cutouts for flannelboard use. Then place five letters on your flannelboard. Have youngsters name the letters on the board. Then, while students cover their eyes, remove a letter. Recite the rhyme shown and then have students name the missing letter. Play several rounds of this entertaining game.

Hocus-pocus, shimmery shoe,
Which little letter did I take from you?

Alphabet Everywhere!

Have youngsters look at the wordless picture book *Alphabet City* by Stephen T. Johnson. In this book, natural and manmade objects form the letters of the alphabet. Prompt youngsters to notice the letter in each picture. Next, grab your digital camera and take students on a walk outside the school. Invite youngsters to find objects that look like letters, such as two branches of a tree forming the letter *Y*. Take a photograph of each letter found. Then place the photos along with corresponding letter cards in an album.

Melissa Vervinck, Somerset Early Childhood Center, Rochester Hills, MI

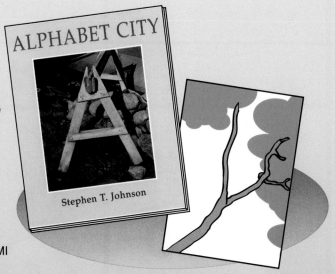

ALPHABET CITY

Stephen T. Johnson

Picture Cards
Use with "Bear's Belly" on page 227.

TEC41037

TEC41037

TEC41037

TEC41037

TEC41037

TEC41037

TEC41037

TEC41037

TEC41037

TEC41037

TEC41037

TEC41037

MATH UNITS

Counting

With the
Three Little Pigs

Read aloud your favorite version of this traditional tale. Then guide youngsters through these fun learning opportunities designed to build counting skills!

ideas contributed by Tricia Brown, Bowling Green, KY

I'm the big bad wolf
And I'm here to say,
"Let me come in.
I promise to stay!"
If you don't,
You know what then?
I'll huff and puff and count to ten!

Huff and Puff!
Counting in proper sequence to ten

Little ones pretend to be wolves during this nifty activity! After reading the story, encourage each youngster to make his scariest wolf face and show his claws as you recite the rhyme shown. At the end of the rhyme, lead your little pack of wolves in counting to ten. Then have each wolf huff and puff to blow down a little pig's house!

A Trio of Pigs
Recognizing numbers to 3

Cut out one copy of the pig pattern on page 233 for each student, plus three extras. Label each pig with a number from 1 to 3. Display three cutouts, each showing a different number, and lead the class in naming the number on each pig. Then give each child one of the remaining cutouts. Tell little ones to listen carefully as you reread the story. As each little pig enters the story, have youngsters with the corresponding pigs hold them in the air and give the appropriate number of oinks.

Blown Away!
Understanding the concept of zero

Make three copies of the house pattern from page 234. Display the houses and have the class count to determine that there are three. Then lead youngsters in reciting the rhyme shown. At the end of the rhyme, have each child blow as hard as she can while you whisk one house out of sight with great dramatic flair! Repeat the process and continue in the same manner as before until all of the houses have been blown away. Then lead youngsters to understand that there are no houses left, and the number used to describe this is zero.

Piggy had a house today,
But the mean old wolf blew it away!

Pig Tails
Counting objects to five

Cut a supply of pink paper strips. Demonstrate for students how to wrap a paper strip around a pencil and then slide the paper off of the pencil to create a curly pig tail. Next, have each child count out five paper strips. Have her use one of the paper strips to make a pig tail and then glue the pig tail to a sheet of construction paper. Encourage her to continue until she has used all five paper strips to create a pretty pink collage of tails. Then have her recount the tails as she points to each one.

Amy Durrwachter
Kirkwood Early Childhood Center
Kirkwood, MO

Sticks and Straw
Comparing sets

When the wolf blew down the pigs' houses, it made a terrible mess! Cut unequal numbers of brown paper strips (sticks) and yellow paper strips (straw) to make a class supply. Gather two containers and label them as shown. Scatter the strips on the floor and tell students that the destruction of the pigs' houses has made quite a mess. Have each child help clean up by picking up a strip and placing it in the corresponding container. Dump out the strips and guide students in counting the sticks and pieces of straw. Finally, help youngsters compare the numbers using the words *less* and *more*.

Wild and Woolly Math

Your little ones will have a roaring good time with these creative math ideas!

1, 2, 3, 4, 5.

Toss and Count
Counting

Youngsters develop gross-motor skills with this whole-group counting activity. Have youngsters stand in a circle; then invite a child to roll a jumbo die. Encourage students to count the number of dots aloud as they jump a corresponding number of times. Prompt the student to give the die to his neighbor. Then continue in the same way, each time using a different movement, such as toe tapping, clapping, and leg patting.

Cathy Mansfield
The Playstation
Trucksville, PA

Take a Guess!
Estimating

A large container and some parental involvement are all you need to add excitement to estimating! Send home with a youngster a see-through, lidded container and a note similar to the one shown. When the container is returned, encourage each youngster to estimate the number of items inside. Record students' responses on a chart and discuss which estimates are highest and lowest. Then have the group help you count aloud to find the actual number of objects. Challenge students to compare the estimates on the chart to the actual number of items in the container. Then send the container and note home with a different youngster.

Cindy Kelley
St. Bernard School
Wabash, IN

Dear Family,
This is our preschool estimation container! Please help your child place a small number of objects (no more than 30) in the container. Make sure all the objects are the same or similar. For example, macaroni, toothpicks, or plastic spoons would be fine but a mixture of the items would not. Then return the container to school with your child.

Thanks a bunch!
Ms. Kelley

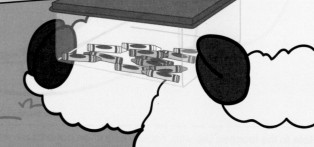

244

Colorful Bands
Patterning

To prepare, gather a supply of baby hair ties in various colors. Place the hair ties in a container and put the container at a center. A child slides these tiny hair ties on her index fingers to create simple patterns. Then she reads the patterns aloud. Now that's simple and fun!

Jodie Tamm
Even Start Family Literacy
Appleton, WI

Totally Tubular
Ordering by size

Cut cardboard tubes into different lengths and then place the tube pieces at a center. A youngster visits the center and stands the pieces in a row from smallest to largest. If time permits, he scrambles the pieces and then arranges them from largest to smallest.

Janet Boyce, Cokato, MN

So Many Socks!
Counting

No doubt you'll hear lots of giggles during this fun and silly activity! Gather a supply of clean, adult-size tube socks. Place the socks in a basket. Gather youngsters in a circle and invite a volunteer to sit in the center of the circle with the basket. At your signal, have the child pull on as many socks as she can, one over the other, on the same foot. After a designated amount of time, have her stop. Then encourage her to remove the socks from her foot one at a time as the class counts aloud.

Peggy Wieck
Litchfield Prekindergarten
Litchfield, IL

245

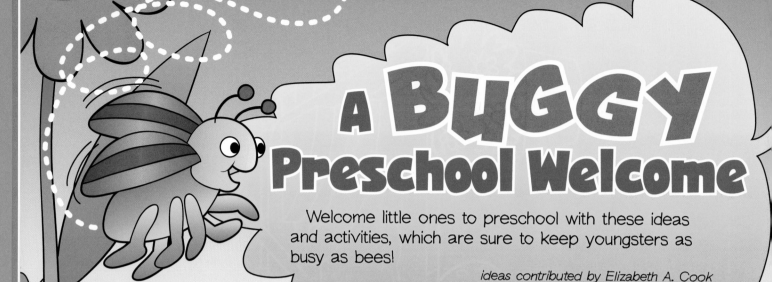

A BUGGY
Preschool Welcome

Welcome little ones to preschool with these ideas and activities, which are sure to keep youngsters as busy as bees!

ideas contributed by Elizabeth A. Cook
King of King's Lutheran School, Mason, OH

Spot Who's Here Today!
Attendance display

Who's in preschool today? You can find out at a glance with this attractive display! In advance, attach an oversize ladybug cutout to your wall. Attach a class supply of Velcro fasteners (loop side only) to the ladybug. If desired, title the display "Spot Who's Here Today!" During your open house or on the first day of school, take a photograph of each youngster. Trim around each youngster's head and then attach it to a black construction paper circle. Laminate the circles for durability and attach the hook side of a Velcro fastener to each circle. Place the resulting spots faceup on a table. When youngsters arrive, have each child find his spot and then attach it to the ladybug.

The Buzz on Names
Getting acquainted game

Color and cut out a copy of the bee pattern on page 255 and laminate it for durability. Gather youngsters in a circle and give a child the bee. As youngsters pass the bee around the circle, prompt them to chant the rhyme shown. When the rhyme ends, have the child holding the bee say his name and then have the remaining youngsters repeat his name. Continue in the same way for several rounds of this game. To add variety to the activity, substitute the underlined words with one of the suggestions and then prompt the children to say the name as described.

Bumblebee, bumblebee, what's your name?
Say it [really loud] and we'll do the same!

Suggested substitutions: *really soft, really silly, really squeaky, really high, really low*

Lots of Jobs

Classroom job display

To make this adorable display, attach a vinyl tablecloth to a board. Then cut out a class supply of construction paper ants (pattern on page 256) and personalize them. Also cut out enough construction paper copies of the cake slice pattern on page 256 to have one for each desired classroom job. Label the slices with the appropriate jobs and then attach them to the board along with the title "Classroom Jobs Take the Cake!" To assign a job to a child, simply attach her ant below the slice of cake.

Janeen Welch
Bates-Rich Beginnings Child Care Center
Fairport, NY

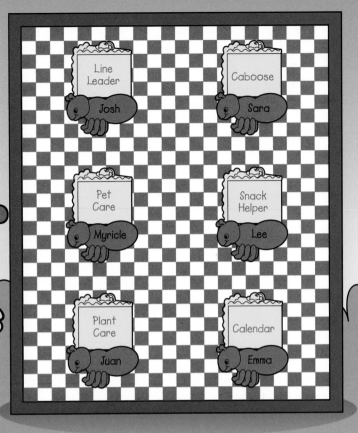

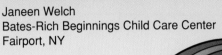

Build a Caterpillar

Nametags

Personalize a tagboard rectangle for each youngster and punch a hole in each resulting nametag. When youngsters arrive for the first day of school, use a safety pin to attach the appropriate nametag to each child's shirt and then attach a colorful sticky dot to the left side of each nametag. Continue in a similar way each day for the first few days of school, resulting in a line of sticky dots. Then use a fine-tip permanent marker to draw a face, antennae, and legs on the dots to make a caterpillar. If desired, send these nametags home as a pleasant memory of the beginning of the year.

Firefly Fun

Storytime

This classic story emphasizes the importance of belonging to a group. Read aloud Eric Carle's story *The Very Lonely Firefly*. Give each child a copy of the firefly pattern on page 255 and have her color it as desired. Then prompt her to crumple pieces of yellow or gold metallic tissue paper and glue the pieces to her firefly as shown. Don't forget to make a firefly craft for yourself as well. Have youngsters attach their fireflies to a wall. Next, keep your firefly nearby and reread the story. At the end of the story, when the lonely firefly finds its friends, have a youngster attach the remaining firefly craft to the wall to join the others.

Where Does It "Bee-long"?

Familiarizing youngsters with the classroom

Youngsters get to know the classroom with this quick game. Cut out several construction paper copies of the bee pattern on page 255. Then attach the bees to a container. Place a few items from each of your centers in the box. Hold up one of the items and ask, "Busy little bees, where does this belong?" When a youngster correctly identifies where the item is normally stored, give her the item and prompt her to make a buzzing noise as she "flies" the item back to the appropriate location. Continue in the same way with each item in the box. What a fun way to familiarize youngsters with different areas in the classroom.

Linda Tharp
Hickory Child Development Center
Bel Air, MD

Bugs in a Rug

Rhyme

Color and cut out a copy of each of the bug patterns on pages 255–257. Gather youngsters in a circle and then place a piece of felt on the floor so it resembles a rug. Lead youngsters in performing the chant shown, having them help you move the props and complete the actions as indicated.

Five little bugs are sitting on a rug.   *Show five fingers.*
One is the bee. Buzz, buzz, buzz!   *Place the bee on the rug.*
Two is the firefly. Blink, blink, blink!   *Place the firefly on the rug.*
Three is the ant. Work, work, work!   *Place the ant on the rug.*
Four is the grasshopper. Hop, hop, hop!   *Place the grasshopper on the rug.*
Five is the butterfly. Flap, flap, flap!   *Place the butterfly on the rug.*
Now five bugs are snug,   *Roll up the rug and bugs.*
All rolled up in a rug!   *Roll forearms around each other.*

254

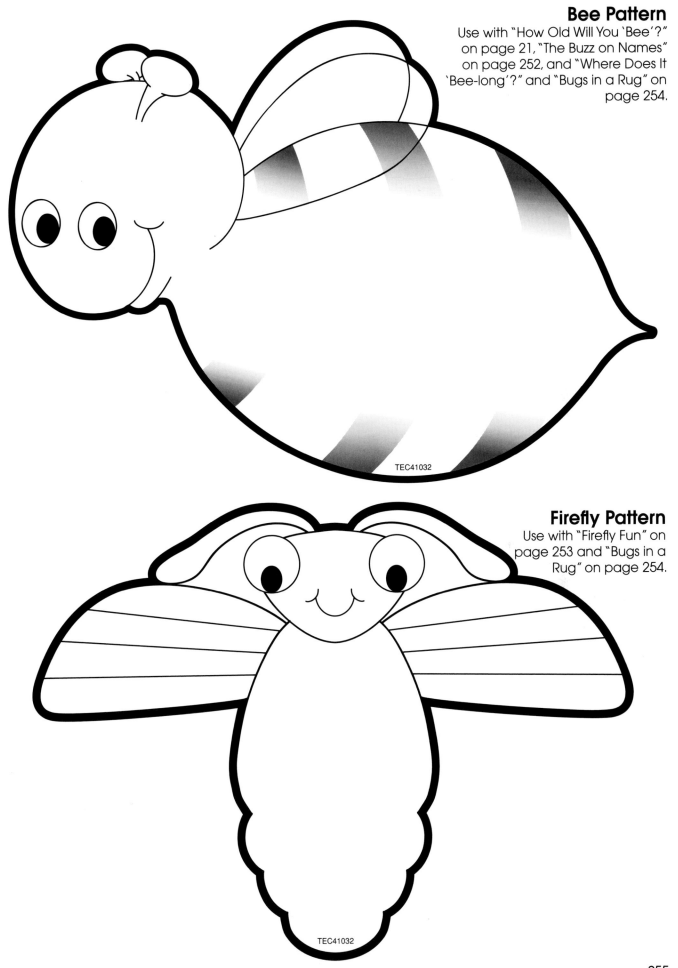

Bee Pattern
Use with "How Old Will You 'Bee'?"
on page 21, "The Buzz on Names"
on page 252, and "Where Does It
'Bee-long'?" and "Bugs in a Rug" on
page 254.

TEC41032

Firefly Pattern
Use with "Firefly Fun" on
page 253 and "Bugs in a
Rug" on page 254.

TEC41032

Ant Pattern
Use with "Lots of Jobs" on page 253
and "Bugs in a Rug" on page 254.

TEC41032

Cake Slice Pattern
Use with "Lots of Jobs" on
page 253.

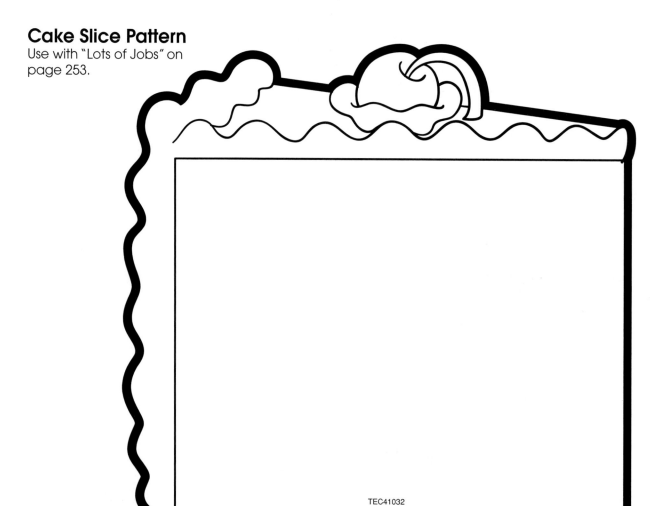

TEC41032

256

TEC41032

TEC41032

Needs of Living Things

Youngsters focus on the needs of living things with this "paws–itively" adorable collection of pet–themed ideas!

ideas contributed by Lucia Kemp Henry, Fallon, NV

What Do They Need?

Here's a toe-tapping tune that will help little ones remember a pet's needs! Color and cut out a copy of the pet patterns on pages 260 and 261. Lead youngsters in singing the song shown. Next, invite a child to choose one of the pet cutouts and attach it to your board. Then lead youngsters in singing another round of the song, substituting the underlined word with the name of the pet chosen. (You may wish to explain that the fish gets air from the water it lives in.) Continue in the same way with each remaining pattern.

(sung to the tune of "Looby Loo")

A [pet] is a living thing.
A [pet] needs a lot of care.
A [pet] needs a nice, safe home.
A [pet] needs food, water, and air.

A Needs Booklet

To make this cute booklet, give each child a construction paper copy of pages 262 and 263. Read each page aloud. Then have each student glue crumpled blue tissue paper to page 1 to resemble water and torn brown paper to page 2 to resemble food. Instruct her to draw a roof on the dog's house on page 3 and attach a heart sticker (or cutout) to page 4. Help her cut out the pages and then staple them in order between two covers.

A pet needs water. 1

A pet needs food. 2

A pet needs a home. 3

A pet needs love. 4

258

Pampered Pets

Spotlight pets' needs with this pet shop dramatic-play area! Gather a variety of stuffed animals, such as cats, dogs, rabbits, and mice. Place the animals in your dramatic-play area along with lidless boxes, shredded paper, small blankets, and plastic bowls. Provide access to a cash register, paper, and crayons, as well as grooming items such as brushes and a plastic tub. Youngsters visit the center to care for the pets and sell them to deserving customers.

Feed the Fish

Youngsters provide food for these crafty goldfish! Place a rectangle of blue bulletin board paper on a table so that it resembles a fish aquarium. Have each child use tempera paint to make several fingerprints at the bottom of the aquarium to resemble gravel. Then have her press a fish-shaped sponge into a shallow pan of orange tempera paint and make a print above the gravel. After each youngster has had a chance to add to the project, tell students that it's time to feed the fish. Spread glue at the top of the aquarium and then give each child an opportunity to shake multicolored glitter (fish food) over the glue. Look at all those happy fish!

Shelter for Spot

This reading area resembles a shelter for man's best friend! Cut an opening in a large piece of cardboard so that it resembles the opening of a doghouse. If desired, have students paint the cardboard. After students choose a dog's name, write the name over the door. Attach the cardboard to a small table and then drape a blanket over the table. Place a variety of pet-themed books in the resulting doghouse as well as a stuffed animal dog and a blanket. What a cozy place to read about pets' needs!

Audrey Englehardt
Meadowbrook Elementary
Moro, IL

SPOT

TEC41032

TEC41032

TEC41032

Booklet Pages 1 and 2

Use with "A Needs Booklet" on page 258.

A pet needs food.

2

A pet needs water.

1

4

A pet needs love.

A pet needs a home. 3

Daytime and Nighttime

Rise and shine! Youngsters will be wide awake and ready to learn with this selection of activities on daytime and nighttime.

Setting the Scene

Developing fine-motor skills

Here's an eye-catching display that's sure to get little ones thinking about daytime and nighttime! Make a supersize sun cutout and moon cutout from poster board. Invite youngsters to decorate the sun with orange and red tissue paper squares and the moon with iridescent cellophane squares. (Be sure to have youngsters decorate both sides of the cutouts.) Suspend the finished sun and moon on opposite sides of your classroom. Then suspend cloud crafts around the sun and star crafts around the moon.

Marie E. Cecchini, West Dundee, IL

Catch a Falling Star!

Identifying colors and shapes

This engaging game is also an excellent time filler! To make a simple falling star beanbag, make two identical felt star cutouts. Hot-glue the cutouts together along their edges, leaving an opening. Place a supply of beans, as well as the ends of several lengths of colorful curling ribbon, in the star. Then hot-glue the opening closed. Gather color and shape flash cards. To begin, identify a child by name and tell him to catch the falling star. Toss the star to the youngster. Then hold up a card. Help the child identify the color or shape on the card. Then have the child toss the star back to you. Repeat the process with a different child.

Janet Boyce, Cokato, MN

264

Pajama Day

Celebrate nighttime with a theme day! Send home with youngsters a note inviting them to wear pajamas and bring flashlights to school on a specific day. Set up several nighttime-themed activities, such as those found in this unit, for this special day. See additional suggestions below for possible activities.

Possible activities:
- "Good Night!" activity on page 270
- "Just Hanging Around" center on page 38
- Sleep-themed read-alouds, such as those shown
- Art activities that use glitter (stardust) or glow-in-the-dark paint
- Flashlight games, such as using flashlights to illuminate letters or shapes displayed in the classroom

Marie E. Cecchini, West Dundee, IL
Jennifer Shea, West Glenville Christian Nursery School, Amsterdam, NY
Marisa Sparks, Mansfield Elementary, Mansfield, LA

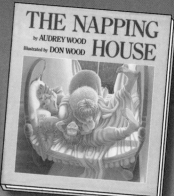

Sun, Moon, and Stars
Reciting a chant

Once youngsters learn this simple action chant, they can easily perform it on their own!

Here is the sun; it's big and bright.	*Put arms over head to make sun.*
And here is the moon, with its glowing light.	*Use hands to make a circle.*
Here are the stars up in the sky,	*Point upward.*
Twinkling brightly way up high.	*Flutter fingers.*

Deborah Garmon
Groton, CT

See the Light!
Developing observation skills

In advance, make several sun cutouts. At the beginning of your school day, have students observe areas of the room where they can see the rays of the sun. Have students help you tape the sun cutouts in those locations. Near the end of the day, have students observe the sun cutouts again, prompting them to notice that many cutouts are no longer in the sunshine. Ask students why the cutouts are no longer in the sunshine, and encourage them to share their thoughts.

Keely Peasner
Liberty Ridge Head Start
Bonney Lake, WA

Awesome Owls!

"Whoooo" will enjoy these owl-themed activities? Why, your little ones will, that's who!

Good Night!
Investigating living things

Youngsters investigate the lifestyles of owls with this active idea! Explain to youngsters that owls are *nocturnal,* which means they sleep during the day and are awake at night. Encourage youngsters to pretend to be owls at nighttime. Turn the lights out in the classroom and prompt students to sing the first verse of the song below as they "fly" about the room. Next, turn on the lights; then have youngsters pretend to be asleep as you sing the remaining verse of the song. Play several rounds of this fun activity!

(sung to the tune of "Good Night, Ladies")

It is nighttime.
It is nighttime.
It is nighttime
When owls fly around.

It is daytime.
It is daytime.
It is daytime
When owls go to sleep.

Shelley Hoster
Jack and Jill Early Learning Center
Norcross, GA

Frequent Flier
Expressing oneself through arts and crafts

Mix a batch of plaster of paris according to the instructions. Have a child help you pour some of the plaster onto a small plastic plate. Prompt the child to place bubble wrap over the plaster, pressing down lightly. When the plaster has hardened slightly, have him remove the bubble wrap. The resulting bumps in the plaster will look similar to the moon's craters. After the plaster has hardened completely, carefully remove it from the plate. Allow the youngster to brush glue over the resulting moon and sprinkle glitter over the glue. Then have her color an owl cutout (patterns on page 273) and glue it to the front of the moon.

Bobbi Chapman, Fiddlesticks Cooperative Preschool, Centralia, WA

Big Eyes

Contributing to a game

Here's a neat twist on the traditional I Spy game. Make a brown construction paper copy of the owl mask on page 272. Cut out the eyeholes and then attach the mask to a jumbo craft stick. Give the mask to a youngster and prompt him to peek through the mask and take note of an object in the classroom and its color. Then encourage him to say, "The owl spies with its really big eyes something that is the color [color name]." When a student guesses the correct object, give the mask to a different student. Then play another round of the game!

Adrianne Hobbs, Mooresville, NC

So Sleepy!

Performing a song

Lead youngsters in performing this cute little owl song!

(sung to the tune of "Are You Sleeping?")

Are you sleeping? Are you sleeping,
Mister Owl, Mister Owl?

You sleep in the daytime
And fly in the nighttime,
When you see perfectly!

Throw arms out to sides.
Form circles with each index finger
and thumb to make eyes.
Pretend to be asleep.
Flap arms.
Form circles with each index finger
and thumb to make eyes.

Deborah Garmon
Groton, CT

Owl Babies

Responding to a story through arts and crafts

Read aloud the story *Owl Babies* by Martin Waddell. At the end of the story, prompt students to compare the appearance of the mother owl and the baby owls, leading them to notice that the baby owls appear white and fluffy, while the mother owl appears brown and feathery. Next, each student glues a strip of brown construction paper to a sheet of black construction paper to make a tree branch. She glues three balls of cotton batting above the branch. Then she glues construction paper eyes, beaks, and feet to the batting so they resemble the three owls in the story. She adds a moon cutout and star stickers to finish the project.

Keely Peasner, Liberty Ridge Head Start, Bonney Lake, WA

Wonderful Winter

Snow, icicles, warm cozy clothing—signs of winter are everywhere! Little ones are sure to love this blizzard of ideas just perfect for the winter season.

Winter Is Here!
Singing a song
Celebrate the arrival of winter with this jaunty little tune!

(sung to the tune of "My Bonnie Lies Over the Ocean")

The leaves from the trees have all fallen.
The branches stand bare in the night.
The snowflakes are making huge piles.
My boots are all covered in white.
Winter, winter, winter is finally here—it's here!
Winter, winter, winter is finally here!

C. Welwood
Learning Experience
Calgary, Alberta, Canada

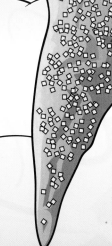

Amazing Icicles
Developing fine-motor skills
No doubt youngsters have noticed lovely icicles hanging from trees and buildings. To begin, show youngsters photos of icicles or bring a real icicle indoors for students to observe. Next, invite students to make their own icicles! Give each child a length of aluminum foil and show him how to mold the foil to make an icicle. Invite students to paint their icicles with slightly diluted glue and then sprinkle iridescent glitter over the glue. When the glue dries, hang the icicles around the classroom.

Mary Davis
Keokuk Christian Academy
Keokuk, IA

It's Snowing!
Following directions

Draw a partially open mouth on a paper plate for each child. Then have her color the plate and draw a nose and eyes to complete the face. Glue cotton balls around the plate so they resemble a hood. Have each child glue a mini snowflake cutout to a tongue cutout. Next, help each child cut a slit in the mouth, slide the tongue into the slit, and then tape the tongue in place. If desired, display these crafts with the title "Let It Snow!"

Shelley Hope
Patterson Kennedy Elementary
Dayton, OH

Snowballs!
Measuring

White makeup pads make perfect snowballs! Gather a supply of inexpensive circular makeup pads and place them in a container. After showing youngsters how to measure objects with the snowballs, place the container in a center. Then invite youngsters to take the container around the room during center time to measure different objects. This block is five snowballs long!

adapted from an idea by Nancy Foss
Wee Care Preschool
Galion, OH

perfect hat.   1

A Hat for
MINERVA
LOUISE

᷒ʸ Janet Morgan Stoeke

Winter Wear
Developing book awareness

In the book *A Hat for Minerva Louise* by Janet Morgan Stoeke, Minerva the chicken tries on several unique hats to wear on a snowy day. After a read-aloud of this book, have students continue the theme of the story with this cute booklet! Make a copy of pages 281 and 282 and the cards on page 283 for each child. Have each youngster color the booklet pages and the cards; then encourage her to cut out the cards and glue one card above each chicken on the first three pages. On the final page, prompt the child to draw above the chicken what she considers to be the perfect hat. When the glue is dry, help her cut out the booklet pages and bind them together behind a cover titled "The Perfect Hat."

No Cavities Here!

Developing fine-motor skills

Incorporate small pieces of black craft foam into white play dough and then form the play dough into large tooth shapes. Place these supersize teeth at a center along with tweezers and an empty plastic container. If desired, provide access to white dress shirts (dental lab coats) and dental face masks. A child puts on a coat and a mask, uses the tweezers to remove the cavities from the teeth, and places the cavities in the container.

Paula Grimes, West Bay Children's Center, Warwick, RI

Brush, Floss, Rinse

Developing healthy habits

For this whole-group activity, have students pretend to be teeth as they stand in a circle with their shoulders touching. Stand in the middle of the circle with the following props: a brush-style ice scraper (toothbrush), a feather boa (dental floss), and a spray bottle of water (rinsing water). Explain the proper way to brush teeth as you pretend to brush the youngsters with the ice scraper. Then floss between the students by wiggling the boa between the youngsters. For a final rinse, use the spray bottle to mist the youngsters. What a fun, memorable activity!

Kimberly Howells, Chatham Elementary, Pittsburgh, PA

Super Smiles

Making a connection between spoken and written words

Youngsters show off their healthy teeth and splendid smiles with this class book activity! Take a photograph of each youngster's smile. Then have each child glue her photo to a sheet of construction paper programmed with the question shown. Have her describe what makes her smile while you write her words and name below the photo. Bind the finished pages together under a cover titled "Super Smiles."

Kathy Ellington, Cedar Creek School, Ruston, LA

What makes me smile?

My cat makes me smile.

Tara

Water Is the Winner!

Developing prediction and observation skills

To begin, have students observe two white hard-boiled eggs and describe what they see. Lead youngsters to conclude that the eggs are white just like their teeth. Next, place one egg in a container of water and the second egg in a container of brown soda. Ask youngsters what they think will happen to the eggs. After the eggs have sat overnight, have students watch as you remove the eggs. *(The egg from the soda will be brown and the egg from the water will be white.)* Ask students to describe what will happen to their white teeth if they drink too much soda. Finally, have students remove the brown stains by gently brushing the egg with a toothbrush topped with toothpaste.

Tracy Hagen, Eagle Bluff Kindergarten Center, Onalaska, WI

A Toothy Tune

Performing an action song

Get youngsters up and moving with this grin-inducing action song. Lead students in singing the song and pantomiming the actions described.

(sung to the tune of "Peanut Butter and Jelly")

First, you get the toothpaste and you squeeze it, you squeeze it!
First, you get the toothpaste and you squeeze it, you squeeze it!

Chorus:
For your healthy, healthy smile, your smile!
Healthy, healthy smile, your smile!

Additional verses:
Then you wet the brush with the water, the water.
You put it on your teeth and you brush them, you brush them.
Then you take some water and you swish it, you swish it.
When you're done with swishing then you spit it, you spit it.

Shelley Hoster, Jack & Jill Early Learning Center, Norcross, GA

Song Cards
Use with "A Sparkly Smile" on page 285.

A Sparkly Smile

(sung to the tune of "I'm a Little Teapot")

I'm a happy smile; just look at me!
I'm white and sparkly, as you can see.
I take care to brush my teeth each day
So cavities will stay away.

©The Mailbox • February/March 2008

A Sparkly Smile

(sung to the tune of "I'm a Little Teapot")

I'm a happy smile; just look at me!
I'm white and sparkly, as you can see.
I take care to brush my teeth each day
So cavities will stay away.

©The Mailbox • February/March 2008

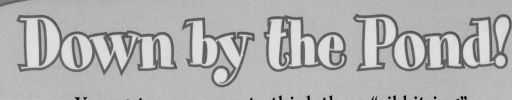

Down by the Pond!

Youngsters are sure to think these "ribbit-ing" pond ideas are just ducky!

What's in the Box?

Building excitement for the unit

Grab youngsters' attention with a box full of mystery items! In advance, place in a lidded container a variety of pond-related items, such as a book, a bag of fish crackers, and a class supply of frog stickers and lily pad cutouts. To begin, display the box and have students predict its contents. Then remove the lid and display the items. After youngsters guess the unit theme, have each child attach a frog sticker to his lily pad. Then read aloud the book as youngsters munch on fish crackers.

Erin McGinness
Great New Beginnings Early Learning Center
Newark, DE

A Pool Pond

Developing an independent interest in books

Youngsters can ponder picture books in this easy-to-make reading center! Place a blue blanket in an empty wading pool to make the pond. To have students make cattails, encourage a child to glue squares of crumpled tissue paper to a small cardboard tube. Roll a piece of construction paper and slide it into each tube. Then staple the tubes in place and attach leaf cutouts. Insert each cattail into a weighted bucket and arrange the buckets around the pond. As your unit progresses, have each child remove his cattail and glue cotton batting over the brown tissue paper to resemble a mature cattail releasing fluffy white seeds.

Laura Kessler, Stoneridge Elementary School, Roseville, CA
Camelia Kline, Kid's-R-Special, Fairmont, WV

Egg, Tadpole, Frog

Developing fine-motor skills

Spotlight the life cycle of a frog with this engaging mural! Trim a piece of blue bulletin board paper into a pond shape and place it on a protected surface. After youngsters have been introduced to the life cycle of a frog, have them visit the pond. To make frog eggs, have each child make a white print of Bubble Wrap cushion material on the pond. Then instruct her to use a cotton swab to make black dots on the print. Next, give her a sponge trimmed into a tadpole shape and encourage her to make green tadpole prints on the pond. Finally, instruct her to glue a frog cutout to the pond as well. Display the finished mural in your classroom.

Debbie Ronga
Sunshine Nursery School
Arlington, MA

Dabbling Ducks

Investigating living things

In advance, cut several plastic cups in half. Glue a strip of craft foam to each pair of cup halves as shown. Place plastic plants in your water table. Then place the duck bill props nearby. To begin, read aloud *In the Small, Small Pond* by Denise Fleming. When you're finished with the read-aloud, revisit the page that shows the diving ducks. Explain to students that the ducks flip upside down in order to reach the water plants they like to eat. Then invite each student to visit the center and place a hand in a duck bill prop as shown. Encourage her to dip her duck bill in the water and pull up some tasty plants, allowing the extra water to drain out of her bill.

Maureen E. Cesari
Raleigh, NC

292

Counting Cattails

Identifying and ordering numbers

Embellish ten jumbo craft sticks, as shown, so they resemble cattails. Write a different number from 1 to 10 on each cattail. Then place the cattails at a center along with a number line and pan with blue play dough (pond). A child identifies the number on each cattail. Then she arranges them in the pond in number order, using the number line as a guide.

Cathy Patterson, The Learning Center of Westerville
Westerville, OH

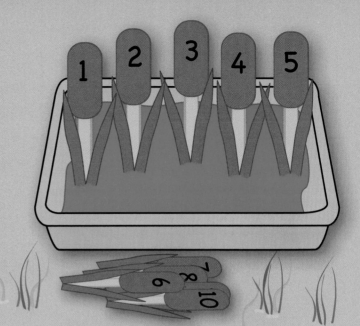

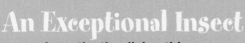

Moving and Grooving!

Developing gross-motor skills

Gather three different instruments, such as a drum, rhythm sticks, and maracas. Play the drum, encouraging students to crawl like turtles. Play the rhythm sticks, prompting youngsters to hop like frogs. Then play the maracas, having students "fly" around the room like dragonflies. Say, "Cattails!" at random times, prompting students to stop the current motion and stand straight and still as if they were cattails. To get youngsters moving again, play one of the instruments.

Courtney Pate, Burlington, NC

An Exceptional Insect

Investigating living things

Explain to youngsters that many different insects live in a pond and one very interesting insect is called a pond skater (or water strider). The pond skater moves on top of the water as if it were skating. Share with youngsters a photograph of a pond skater. Next, encourage each student to use a permanent marker to draw a simple pond skater on a craft foam oval. Have him place his pond skater in a pan of water and then touch it lightly. It skates across the pond just like a real pond skater!

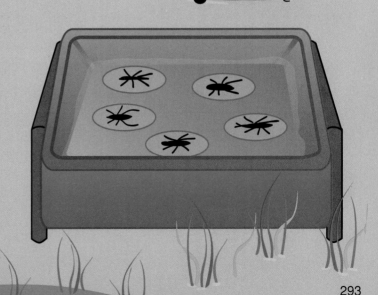

Peek in the Pond

**Making connections between spoken
and written words**

Have each child color a copy of pages 295 and 296 as desired. Read aloud the text on each booklet page, prompting him to supply the name for each pond critter as you write each word in the appropriate space. For the final page, have him name and then draw a different pond critter. Help the child cut out the pages and staple them to a cover labeled as shown. Round the corners of the booklet. Then attach eye cutouts and green sticky dots to embellish the project.

A Beaver Lodge

Following directions

To make this simple beaver lodge snack, melt chocolate chips and butterscotch chips in a microwave to resemble the mud used to make a lodge. Cool the mixture slightly. Then have children help you mix logs (chow mein noodles) with the mud. A child places a spoonful of the mixture on waxed paper. When the snacks have hardened, she places her snack in a dollop of blue-tinted vanilla pudding so it resembles a beaver lodge in a pond. Yum!

Betty Selchert, Alcester-Hudson Preschool, Alcester, SD

Who Is Lost?

Sorting

Some of these critters don't belong in a pond! Place blue bulletin board paper (or a blue blanket) on the floor so it resembles a pond. Gather cards that show both pond dwellers and animals that do not live in a pond. Then place the cards on the pond. Have a student find an animal that does not belong in a pond. Help him name where the animal does make its home and set the card aside. Continue in the same manner until only pond animals are left in the pond!

Courtney Pate, Burlington, NC

_____ live in the pond.

1

_____ live in the pond.

2

_____ live in the pond.

3

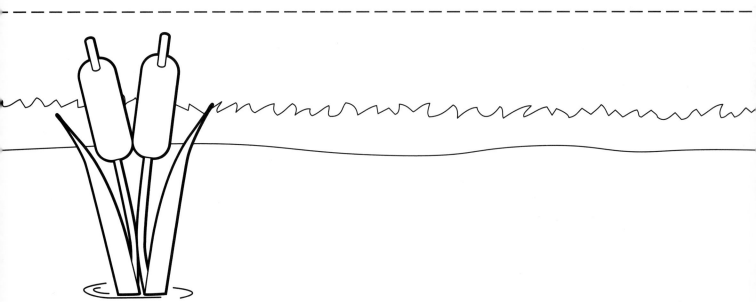

Who else lives in the pond?

4

Get to Know Community Helpers!

Who Works at School?

Begin your community helpers unit by studying workers right in your own school! Take youngsters to visit school workers, such as your school director, counselor, librarian, and cafeteria staff. Have the workers share what they do and what tools they use. When you come back to the classroom, have students discuss what they saw, heard, and smelled while you record their words on a chart similar to the one shown.

Eve Dutkiewicz, Chavez Learning Station, Kenosha, WI
Susan Luengen, Makalapa Elementary School, Honolulu, HI

We went to visit the cafeteria staff.		
We saw...	We heard...	We smelled...
food	a mixer	pizza
a spoon	a refrigerator	
a plate		
an oven		

A Helper Song

Gather a community helper cutout for of the professions shown; then attach the hook side of a Velcro fastener to the back of each cutout and place them near your flannelboard. Lead youngsters in singing the song shown. Then have a child find the appropriate community helper and attach it to the flannelboard. Continue in the same way with the remaining verses shown.

(sung to the tune of "The Muffin Man")

Do you know who [brings us mail]?
Who [brings us mail]? Who [brings us mail]?
Do you know who [brings us mail]?
What is this worker's name?

Continue with the following verses:
puts out fires
keeps us safe
makes us well
helps us learn

adapted from an idea by Sheri Church
Wiggles & Giggles Childcare Center
Boone, NC

Health Care Collage

In advance, attach compact discs to separate head-bands so they resemble doctors' headlamps. Then place the headlamps at a table along with paper and a variety of health care collage items, such as cotton balls, tongue depressors, cotton swabs, bandages, and gauze. Invite each child to visit the center and don a headlamp. Then prompt him to attach items to a sheet of paper to make a health care collage!

Liz Alford, Red River Elementary, Coushatta, LA
Joyce Desmond, Joseph M. Ferraina Early Childhood Learning
   Center, Long Branch, NJ

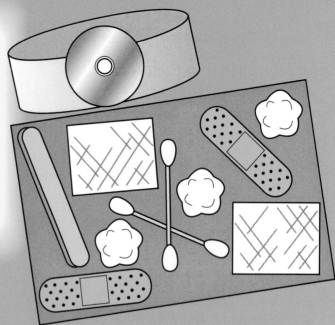

Call a Plumber!

This plumber-themed center develops youngsters' spatial and fine-motor skills! Place a variety of inter-connecting pieces of PVC pipe in a center along with play tools, a phone, bottle brushes, paper, and crayons. Youngsters visit the center and pretend to be plumbers, using the items to fix plumbing problems and write out receipts.

Sue Fleischmann, Waukesha County Project Head Start
Waukesha, WI

Super Sanitation Workers

Gather a variety of empty food boxes and wrappers and place them at a center along with a large poster board trash can cutout (silver poster board looks partic-ularly attractive!). Read aloud the book *Trashy Town* by Andrea Zimmerman and David Clemesha. Then invite students to the center and encourage them to cut out labels and glue them to the trash can to show what is in one of Mr. Gilly's trash cans! As they work, invite them to identify letters that they recognize.

Sue Fleischmann

Preschool Police Academy

Make a supply of page 301 in a variety of skin tones. Also make blue construction paper copies of page 302. Help each child cut out the patterns. Then encourage her to attach a photo of herself to the body cutout as shown. Next, have her glue the clothing and only the top portion of the hat to the body. Help her fold the hat to form a brim. Then instruct her to attach star stickers to the shirt and hat. Display these cute crafts with police shield cutouts naming each of your little officers. Then add the title "Preschool Police Academy."

Kathy Sessions, Cannon Falls, MN

Night Workers, Day Workers

Mount a sheet of black paper and a sheet of white paper on a wall. Then attach star stickers and a sun cutout to the sheets as shown. Have students name jobs and decide whether they are daytime jobs, nighttime jobs, or jobs that people could go to during the daytime and the nighttime. Write the suggested job names on the appropriate papers.

Marie Cecchini
West Dundee, IL

All Business

Delight youngsters with this portable business center! Place in a briefcase a supply of small cards (business cards), notepads, graph paper, a play cell phone, pencils, and a calculator. A youngster takes the briefcase to pretend meetings. If desired, place the briefcase at a table with an old computer keyboard and a play phone. Now your little businessperson has an office!

Norinne Weeks, Carillo Elementary School, Houston, TX

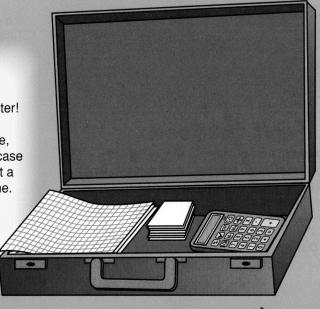

Splendid Snake Skin

Explain to youngsters that snakes shed their skin. Then show students a photograph of a snake's skin or, if possible, share a real snake's shed skin. Give each child a sheet of brown construction paper and encourage her to draw a snake on the paper. Give her a piece of Bubble Wrap cushioning material cut into the shape of a snake. Have her work her fine-motor skills by popping the bubbles on the material. The result looks and feels like a real snake's shed skin! Then have her glue the shed skin next to her snake. If desired, have her glue sticks and other natural items to the paper.

Angela Evans, Crossgates Methodist Children's Center
Brandon, MS

So Many Scales

Melon seed–shaped pasta (or orzo) makes terrific scales for projects at this reptile art center! Place the pasta at a table along with paintbrushes, containers of glue, paint, scissors, and enlarged tagboard copies of the reptiles on page 306. A youngster visits the center and cuts out one of the reptiles. Then she brushes glue on the reptile and presses melon seed–shaped pasta on the glue. When the glue is dry, she brushes paint over the pasta to finish her reptile.

adapted from an idea by Karen E. McMillan
Pima Community College Child Development Center
Tucson, AZ

Did You Know?

A reptile's scales are mostly made of keratin—the same substance found in our hair and fingernails!

ISBN-13: 978-156234857-1
ISBN-10: 156234857-4

9 781562 348571